Seeing the Sacred in Life

A Guide To Living Each Day In The Present

The Practical Spirituality Series

by David D. Dameron

Volume 1
REMEMBERING OUR SPIRIT
Volume 2
SEEING THE SACRED IN LIFE

authorHOUSE™

1663 LIBERTY DRIVE, SUITE 200
BLOOMINGTON, INDIANA 47403
(800) 839-8640
WWW.AUTHORHOUSE.COM

First published by AuthorHouse 09/30/04

ISBN: 1-4184-6645-X (e)
ISBN: 1-4184-6643-3 (sc)
ISBN: 1-4184-6644-1 (dj)

Library of Congress Control Number: 2004097801

Printed in the United States of America
Bloomington, Indiana

This book is printed on acid-free paper.

Table of Contents

For Susan

Acknowledgments

There are several people I want to thank for helping me bring this book to fruition:

My wife, Susan, for being my proofreader and my sanity check and for letting me know whether the writing was making sense.

My editor, Denise Stallcup, who continues to amaze me that she can actually understand what I am trying to say and wordsmiths my text and ideas with great professionalism.

My cover artist, Arthur Douët, who I consider to be one of the finest intuitive artists in the world. If you want to view his artwork, you can visit his website at *www.arthurdouet.com.*

To Jayson Boulet, a wonderful graphic artist, who has helped me get the cover art ready for the publisher on both of my books.

To many friends and clients who submitted stories for me to share in this very public way. Although I could not use all of your stories, I was touched by how Spirit has influenced your life journeys.

Finally, I would like to say that I have made every effort to contact some of you whom I have not seen in years to get your permission to use your stories. If I did use your story without being able to contact you first, I did my best to conceal your identity.

x

If I Had My Life to Do Over

I'd dare to make more mistakes next time * I'd relax
I would limber up * I would be sillier than I have been this trip
I would take fewer things seriously * I would take more chances
I would make more trips * I would climb more mountains and swim
more rivers * I would eat more ice cream and less beans
I would perhaps have more actual troubles, but fewer imaginary ones

You see, I'm one of those people who live sensibly and
sanely hour after hour, day after day. Oh, I've had my
moments. If I had it to do over again, I'd have more of
them. In fact, I'd try to have nothing else.

Just moments, one after another, instead of living so many
years ahead of each day. I've been one of those persons
who never goes anywhere without a thermometer, a hot
water bottle, a raincoat, and a parachute. If I could do it
again, I would travel lighter than I have. If I had my life
to live over, I would start barefoot earlier in the spring and
stay that way later in the fall.

I would go to more dances * I would ride more merry-go-rounds
I would pick more daisies

—Nadine Stair and Elizabeth Lucas

Introduction

"When faced with the need to make tough choices, it's tempting to rely solely on our rational minds and observable facts to help us make decisions, the way most of our cultural training has taught us to do. But I believe that the heart of the personal growth process lies in a willingness to watch for clues coming from beyond the physical realm as well. This means learning to listen for what some would call the still, small voice of God, or the quiet workings of Spirit."

—Rudi Harst, *Hurry Slowly*

Unlimited prosperity. Perfect health. A rewarding career. Peace of mind. Total and complete contentment. I have pursued these states of being consciously for the last twenty-five years of my life. There have been times when they have come with in my reach and I embraced them; at other times they have eluded me.

Yet even when I achieved these things, I still felt an empty space inside of myself—a place where an important piece of my destiny still waited to be fulfilled. I was missing a vital element in my life: that of a committed, soul-connected relationship.

I am not talking about desiring someone in my life because of a perception that I needed to be with a partner, or a fear of being alone. I am referring to a need I came to realize was part of my being, a need to be in a committed partnership and marriage that would be fulfilling on the earthly plane, and spiritually as well. In my mind and in my heart, I envisioned, clearly, what this person embodied and I described her in my journal on October 6, 1998, as though I had already found her, as though we had already met:

> *"She is of Spirit. We recognized each other when our eyes met. There was a feeling—a vibration that we both had been searching for. We had been down many paths to arrive here, and we knew that timing was everything. She is a conscious being who understands the value of true work. She is in pursuit of the truth and explores her many worlds through several spiritual paths.*
>
> *Her outward beauty is only a reflection of that which lives within. She understands me. She feels my emotion and knows how to walk with me. She is creative, and together we realize the power of two and allow space in our togetherness—a love that transcends my own needs.*
>
> *A bond that is not severed over petty desires and expectations. She is a friend to me and to my children, and to other people who are important in my life. I embrace her circle with a joyful awareness and desire to serve her because I respect her and her work and her values and her needs.*
>
> *We join in a physical space that is only matched and exceeded by our desire for union*

with the Divine. We travel the inner planes together. We embrace life by manifesting our desires and His desires. She brings stability to my life because her waters are calm as she is independent, yet desirous of having some of her human needs met. We came together at a perfect time—divinely orchestrated.

We continually find ways to express our gratitude, and we invite Spirit into our lives on a daily basis. We seek to keep our hearts connected even when the ocean becomes rough. We look back with no regrets that we seized the moment and chose love above all other temptations.

I love you, and I invite you into my life. And I give thanks for your spirit because we are Spirit!"

I wrote this ode to my future soul mate one evening as I sat alone in my apartment, listening to a Mozart concerto and sipping a glass of fine wine. It was my own private celebration and toast to my future life partner. I knew, even then, that I would find her.

Just a few months before this evening, I had ended a four-year relationship with a wonderful spirit, but as wonderful as she was, and still is, she was not the one. She was not the soul I was looking for, the one who could touch my heart, my soul, and my spirit.

At that time, I had been divorced for several years. In the years since my divorce, I had met many wonderful women, but my heart kept telling me it wanted something more. So on that fateful night in October, I really opened my heart to the Universe and expressed—with great passion and feeling—that I wanted, beyond all else, to find my soul mate. I desired to build my life on the foundation of a committed partnership and live the rest of my days in a deeply connected relationship and marriage.

Concurrent with this vision I also determined that I was prepared to live the rest of my life alone before I would ever engage in a casual relationship again. I was tired of dating; I wanted to truly experience a soul-connected relationship before I made my transition from this lifetime.

While I knew the power of envisioning what I wanted and telling the Universe I was ready for it, little did I know what I had unleashed that fall evening in a small suburb outside of San Antonio, Texas. From that night, events would unfold at a feverish pace I could never have predicted or imagined.

Looking back, I see that the next few months were somewhat comical in nature. Once I envisioned what I wanted, I became very intent on finding my "twin flame." I knew she was out there and I so looked forward to meeting her at last. Whenever I met new women for the first time, I see now that they wanted to run the other way once I told them my story and what I was searching for. Each of the ladies must have thought I was crazy when I would pose the pointed question that inevitably followed my story: "Are you the one?"

To further complicate things I again came into contact with two women whose talents I have always admired. One woman is an "intuitive" who lives in Baton Rouge, Louisiana. The other is a Jungian astrologer who lives near San Antonio. These individuals are not parlor psychics or newspaper astrologers. They are committed professionals in their respected scientific fields. (Yes, I believe that an informed approach to astrology or psychic abilities qualifies as a science!)

I had readings with each of these women, and they both said almost the same words to me: "You would not believe what is going on in your life right now." Both of them told me that my soul mate would come into my life by the end of June 1999.

The intuitive counselor described my soul mate in detail to me and she even said my soul mate's first name began with the letter S. What neither of them could tell me was how and when she and I were going to meet. I found it interesting that their readings only magnified what I had set in motion that evening in my apartment when I affirmed my intention to bring a soul-committed relationship into my life.

Even so, based on the response I was getting from women I met, I began to wonder how I was going to meet my soul mate when I was scaring new women off with my story and my intent. Should I not say anything, I asked myself, and just let things unfold? But it was hard to take a casual approach when I had rejected the idea of a long-term dating relationship. I didn't want to spend weeks leading up to telling someone I was dating what I was really looking for; I didn't feel I had that time to squander, especially since I'd stated I wanted no more casual dating.

I was comforted that both consultants said my soul mate would recognize me immediately as someone she also was looking for, and that, in fact, we would each recognize the other simultaneously.

I endured a few more months of strained introductions that culminated in the woman running the other way, and fast. Then I entered a phase in which women did not run, but listened and responded positively when I told them about my search. Although I met some wonderful spirits and although each had certain aspects I was looking for in a life partner, each time my heart told me they were not the one I was searching for.

By April of 1999, I was becoming dejected. Where and how was I supposed to meet this mystery woman? Would she be looking for the same thing I was? Would our initial meeting be filled with fireworks, only to fizzle out after really getting to know each other? All of these questions haunted me. Still, I remained committed to my vision and persistently looked for situations in which I could meet new people, new women.

Then one day I received a notice in the mail for an upcoming workshop to be held in June at a resort just outside San Antonio. It was being presented by two good friends of mine, John and Jan Price of the Quartus Foundation. John and Jan are both authors; John has penned over eighteen books on the subjects of spirituality and personal growth. Jan is the author of a book on her near-death experience.

I had taken another of their workshops earlier that year; ironically, the purpose of that workshop had been to teach people how to manifest what they truly wanted in their lives. I had taken the workshop for the express purpose of aiding me in bringing my soul mate into my life.

At the workshop I'd attended, each of the participants was asked to put a symbol of what they wanted to manifest in their lives on a poster on the wall. I had drawn a pair of big, red lips to represent the relationship I wanted to attract into my life.

What I did not realize until later was that my future wife and soul mate was also attending that workshop, but, as we did not interact at that time, we never recognized each other. It was not yet time for us to come together! At this workshop each of us had been more intent on gaining information about our personal issues than we were about meeting someone.

So I ended up taking the June 1999 workshop, as it was on how to attract the relationship you wanted into your life! With that theme I felt it was possible I'd meet my soul mate at the workshop itself, and I was more than ready to try something new to make my vision manifest.

As I filled out the workshop paperwork I wondered what would happen to my enthusiasm if, by the end of June, my soul mate had not appeared. My closest friends told me to be patient; like many people in my life, my friends were convinced this union between my future wife and me was destined to happen.

The day came for the workshop, and looking around the room, I was both heartened and discouraged. Almost all of the participants were women; but unfortunately, most of them were from out of state or were married. I had a preconceived idea that my life partner would, of course, be single, and that she would live in or near San Antonio.

Even so, my eye was drawn again and again to one particular woman who stood out. Her name was Susan, and she and the girlfriend attending the workshop with her were from Kalamazoo, Michigan. It almost makes my heart stop now to remember that I took that as a sign Susan was not the woman for me. I definitely did not envision trying to establish and maintain a long-distance relationship.

As the weekend progressed I made no special effort to talk to Susan, and she and I only spoke a couple of times on the kinds of meaningless issues one has in casual conversation. But on the last day of the workshop I still found myself extremely, strangely attracted to Susan. How, I wondered, could I be so taken with a person with whom I had only spent a few minutes?

On the last day of the workshop, Susan and her friend suggested, in a fun way, that I come up to Michigan sometime and visit them. I indicated that I had an extra airline ticket and I might just do that. Everyone was saying their good-byes to one another in words and hugs, and Susan was the last person I embraced.

In that moment something happened to me—to both of us. It felt a huge surge of electricity between us. I looked into Susan's eyes and I knew she was the one. But I had no way of knowing, at that moment, whether Susan was feeling the same thing. There was no time, as Susan and her friend were driving back to Michigan and had to get started, but I told Susan I would e-mail her in a few days.

My e-mail was waiting for Susan when she arrived in Michigan. It was deliberately non-committal, one of those "how are you doing and how was the trip?" e-mails. The magnitude of my connection with Susan, brief though it was, had changed me from an intent tiger to a skittish pussycat. I was now nervous about my vision and Susan's appearance, and above all I was wondering whether she was feeling, in any way, the same feelings I was. But even without knowing Susan's take on the situation, or on me, I was about to put my heart on the line.

She e-mailed me back, and I e-mailed her, and we continued this casual back-and-forth for a couple of days. Then, at one o' clock in the morning on July 7, I was lying awake and thinking of her when my telephone rang. It was Susan. We talked for a few minutes, and I remember thinking she seemed nervous, when suddenly Susan broke down emotionally and told me that she loved me. She also said she would understand if I felt her feelings weren't reasonable, or if I thought she was moving too fast.

My mind and heart were racing. All of a sudden—after months of speaking with women frightened by my own intensity—I was being confronted by someone moving more quickly, emotionally, than I was.

I was a little stunned at first, but I recognized that my dream had come knocking at last, and I responded in that very special moment that I also loved her.

Beyond its happy ending, the great thing about this story is how similar Susan's story is to mine—it is truly *our* story. She, too, had felt a deep yearning for a soul mate and had been looking, as I had, and for the same reasons. She had consulted with her spiritual advisors and teachers and had been told that her soul mate was going to come into her life, and at this very time.

And now neither of us felt any inclination to be patient. I flew to Kalamazoo at the end of July 1999. I had purchased an engagement ring before leaving San Antonio, and as Susan and I sat on the shores of Lake Michigan at sunset on July 30, 1999, I proposed. She, of course, said yes.

Being somewhat pragmatic people—though you wouldn't guess so from our story—we both look back at this chain of events with some amusement and astonishment. We're still a little surprised at how swept away we were by our emotions and by how quickly we acted on them.

We decided that, because of my kids and the nature of my work, Susan would move to San Antonio. That was not an easy decision for her, since she had lived in Kalamazoo for over forty years. But destiny was with us; her house sold even before the realtors could put the sign in the yard. In the spring of the following year, she was offered a position in San Antonio as a school principal. And on July 7, 2000, Susan and I were married in a four-hundred-year-old church in San Antonio, in the presence of my children, Ben and Amanda.

I tell you this story for two reasons—first, to point out how destiny can tie up a number of complex loose ends with ease; and second, to illustrate that intentions fired by great emotion can move mountains. This story—how it was conceived, how it transpired, and the challenges it presented—is a template for how you can use the book you're holding to bring change and, indeed, miracles to your own life.

Take it from Susan and me—it's never too late to change your life. It took half of our lives, and many experiences, for us to finally find one another. That's why our mantra, from the beginning, has been "No Wasted Time," and we continue to be determined to live *each moment* together to the fullest.

Just as each of us had determined to find our life partner, we decided, after finding one another, what shape our partnership should take. We made a conscious decision not to let differences of opinion or personal styles and habits get in the way of how we felt about one another. This meant talking about any disagreements that came up, working through them, and returning to that joyful and loving space we had both been searching for and which had brought us together.

I have thought many times about those three special words, "No Wasted Time." I've realized what a gift they are; they represent a decision to live life in the present, to its fullest degree, and through them, life is truly filled with happiness and joy. They ensure that, even in challenging times, we will come to understand the gifts of our challenges and enjoy the many opportunities that life affords us, each moment.

Looking back, I see that, in my awkward pursuit to find Susan, questioning each new woman I met, I had asked myself many times how I would find and connect with the woman I'd asked Spirit to send into my life. I worried and fretted: Where would I meet her? Would we recognize one another?

Through this experience, I learned I don't need to concentrate on the "hows" of how something is going to happen. I need only stay in contact with the Source. This book will help you learn to do the same. See the sacred in life! Go to your Divine nature, the source of how things happen. Stay present. Our divinity is responsible for orchestrating our needs. Our only job is to pay attention and follow our intuitive nature. Remember that for every effect, there is a cause! Once you have stated your intent and have connected to it through your passion, the Source will take over and do the rest.

In my first book, *Remembering Our Spirit*, I indicated that it was my belief that we are spiritual beings—we are literally aspects of the Divine who, by the gift of choice, can live a life of fulfillment, a deeply connected and purposeful life, and live in unlimited abundance. Life is a reflection of our choices; one of the strongest lessons I learned from asking for a soul mate and finding Susan is the power of *intention*. When we can envision, clearly, whatever we desire, feel it with great passion, and act on our desire in an appropriate way, then our divinity goes to work to bring that desire into manifestation. What power!

I have entitled this book *Seeing the Sacred in Life* in dedication to my wife who inspires me to live life to the fullest in each moment, as she does. I am thankful to life for having brought us together. If you are wishing to live in peace, joy, and happiness, truly embracing a spiritually fulfilling life, then this book can assist you in your journey, as was the intent of my first book.

Each of my books stands alone; you don't need to have read my first book to understand this book or my future books. This book continues the structure that readers found effective in my first book, and that I hope you will find useful as well.

I recommend you first read through the entire book, then go back and begin to read each chapter again. Each chapter begins with a story that serves to illustrate the power and the uses of the sacred element that is its subject. The story is followed by several short passages to allow you to journal your own thoughts and insights. By meditating on and contemplating each passage, you can begin to establish a connection with your spirit, and understand the power that resides there.

It is in that very special and sacred space—your spirit, your divinity—that you come to appreciate the gifts life has afforded you. You deserve to be happy, fulfilled, and prosperous. You deserve to ask for what you yearn for, and to have your yearnings answered.

Through journaling your insights and feelings, you, in a certain respect, will be writing your own book—the book of your own life and your own potential. Each of us has a purpose in life, and by writing down your insights, you can begin to see the secrets of life, and the path you were meant to follow, unfolding.

It is my hope that this book will touch your spirit, help you realize who you are, and help you to bring forth a deeper awareness of your untapped potential. In doing so, you claim your divinity and the glory, strength, and power that come from that connection.

Throughout the book, one overriding approach to each chapter, each element, ensures your success in bringing spirituality and change into your life: the power of the present—*this very moment*. It is my belief that our divine potential can best emerge when we are totally present in the moment and not focused on past or future events. It is also my belief that only in the present can we see the sacred in life.

One of the great secrets of life that I hope you discover through this book is that what you bring forth into your life already exists—even before your conscious mind conceives of it and before it has manifested in a way you can recognize. This realization became clear to me when Susan and I finally found each other. Though we had attended workshops together, we did not truly see each other until we were ready in our hearts to find our life partner. In other words, until we believed that a partner was waiting for us somewhere, we could not see or recognize that partner.

Another wonderful insight that I learned from this experience was that Susan was not outside of me, she was inside of me, and she had always been there ready for me to discover. Until I could envision Susan, feel her in my heart, and then be vigilant in my daily activities to find her, I did not have the ability to attract her to me. This internal process was the same for Susan—once she stated her intent to find her soul mate and connected to that intent through her passion, she was drawn to me, and I to her.

So let us realize that all things come from Spirit, and let us be thankful for all that has already been given to us. Let us choose to live in the present and never waste a single moment in anger, jealousy, or envy. Let us choose to forgive those who have caused us pain, and let us make a decision from this day forth not only to treat each other with respect and love, but, most of all, to treat ourselves in the same way.

Let us embrace each moment with our conscious intentions filled with compassion and gratitude. I wish each of you peace and enlightenment in your journey and unfolding. My wish for you is that you see and embrace the sacredness of life. Welcome to the present!

CHAPTER 1:

SPIRITUALITY

"Living the spiritual life is not only recognizing the Divine Presence in ourselves—but in EVERYONE. It is considering every person AS their Divine identity, regardless of the situation."

—John Randolph Price, *The Jesus* Code

I cannot begin a book like this one, or begin one of the stories within it, without first talking about God. I cannot suggest to someone how to live a fulfilling life without talking about *first cause*—in other words, the source of all things in our visible universe. Whether you call this force by any of the many names by which it is known—God, Deity, Higher Power, Spirit, or Great Spirit to name a few—it is my contention that there is a Higher Power, and we are intimately connected to that power.

For that reason, this opening chapter explores the subject of a higher force as the basis of spirituality. But before I discuss the subject of spirituality, I am going to share a remarkable story with you.

There have been times in my life when I questioned whether God existed, in spite of all of my reading and research on this subject. Most often, my doubts were caused by challenges I had attracted into my life that made me question or just forget about the existence of a Higher Power.

I now know that my struggles during these times were an attempt to reject truths and lessons I had attracted and brought into my life as a way to help me learn and grow. In questioning the existence of God, I was also avoiding my own responsibility in having created and attracted those truths and lessons. I was struggling with this dynamic, bringing elements into my life that I resisted, and, as a result of my struggle against them, questioning the existence of God, when a single event changed everything for me. In the mid-eighties, I had an experience that changed the course of my life. Because of what happened to me, I never again doubted the existence of a Higher Power.

I was living in San Antonio, Texas, and at that time I had been offered a unique opportunity to become general manager for a small-book press in Northern California. I was married to my first wife, and we had just had a baby boy. After some discussion, my wife and I made the decision to accept the job offer, sell our house and the small bookstore we owned, and move to California.

The move and the new job represented a great opportunity for us, but the change required that we attend to the many details involved in relocating across the country. The first step was to locate housing, and we found a house that seemed suitable in the small, Northern California town, only to find out that the landlords would not allow pets. That provision was completely unacceptable to us, as we had three wonderful dogs that were part of our family.

We began calling about any and all available houses in the area, only to discover that *no one* in the town would allow pets. We were left with a very tough decision: either we would have to turn down this great opportunity, or we would have to find homes for our dogs.

I wrestled with the problem for several days and finally decided that, first and foremost, this move was important for me and my family and I wanted to accept the job offer, whatever it took to do so. I knew that my decision meant giving up the dogs, which would break my heart. The decision also meant I had to somehow find good homes for them, and quickly.

I remember standing in the backyard one spring night in San Antonio, closing my eyes and, with great feeling and passion, asking for help in finding the perfect home for each of our dogs. In my mind's eye, I pictured the perfect new owners being attracted to us and entering our lives, and I pictured us feeling confident that we could entrust our dogs to them.

My final prayer on this matter, and my exact words to my Higher Power, were, "I need a Christmas present in July, Spirit." July was the month in which we would be moving to California. My intention clearly defined and stated, I sprang into action the next day, put an ad in the paper, and began calling close friends to let them know our situation.

A couple of weeks went by, and in the midst of our preparations to move we were called out of town. Our routine was to board our dogs at a great kennel we had found on the outskirts of San Antonio. When we returned to pick up our dogs, I told the kennel owner, a wonderful woman whose whole life revolved around her love for dogs, about our relocation plans and our dilemma with our pets.

With this wonderful glint in her eyes and a smile on her face, the kennel owner asked if I'd let her take our mixed-breed dog, Mona. "I've fallen in love with Mona," the woman confessed. I knew the feeling was mutual; we had always noticed how glad Mona was to be left with this kind woman, and so without hesitation, I told the kennel owner yes.

With tears in our eyes, we left Mona with this wonderful spirit that very day. I remember walking back to the car and saying *thank you* silently to Spirit for answering my prayer and taking care of Mona. This left us to find homes for our remaining dogs, two Brittany spaniels.

Weeks passed, bringing no opportunities to place the dogs. I continued to put ads in the paper. I was especially concerned about our male Brittany, Max, who I knew would have a hard time adjusting to a new home in which he knew no one and had no connection. We were becoming desperate when, one day, we received a call from a gentleman who said he was a breeder of Brittany spaniels. He asked if he could come by to look at Max, and I agreed.

I had devised a rather extensive interview process to ensure we would be placing our dogs in quality homes. But when the gentleman and I met, he exceeded all my hopes and expectations. His family had raised purebred

4

Brittany spaniels for three generations; he had grown up around the dogs and clearly had a love for the breed. Though I knew Max's temperament would make the adjustment hard for him, I couldn't imagine finding a better home for him and could only hope he would, in time, settle in with his new family. I made the decision to let Max go with the gentleman and handed him Max's papers to examine.

Then something happened that reaffirmed my belief in the power and willingness of Spirit to answer our prayers, even beyond what we originally request. When the gentleman saw Max's papers, his jaw dropped and he looked up at me in total astonishment.

He said, "I have something to show you," and pulled out a pedigree on one of the dogs he owned. His next four words shook me to my very being. "I have Max's father," he said. That's right! This man had raised Max's father, and that meant Max would not only be going to a good home, he would be reunited with family and spend the rest of his days with his father.

The gentleman and I both had tears in our eyes over this miraculous turn of events. Without hesitation, we made arrangements for him to pick Max up the next week. I would not have believed I could let Max go with anything but complete sorrow, and yet on the day I watched the breeder drive off with Max, my heart sang with joy. I knew I was going to miss Max very much, but I was deeply grateful to God for bringing me such an amazingly wonderful answer to my prayer.

This left my female Brittany, Penny, who was my first dog and who had a very special place in my heart. I continued putting ads in the paper, but the day of our departure to California was fast approaching with no solution in sight. I was getting nervous about not being able to find a home for Penny, and in spite of the wonderful homes I'd been led to for Mona and Max, I was starting to lose faith that my prayers for Penny would be answered.

Finally, one evening, while taking a walk, I became overwhelmed by my fears for Penny and our situation. Instinctively, I began speaking to Spirit, saying with great emotion how much I had appreciated being able to find a home for Mona and Max. But I told Spirit that I could not move to California without knowing Penny was in a safe place. I repeated my original prayer, saying, "I really need a Christmas present in July."

The very next day I received a call from a woman who said she had seen my ad and really wanted a Brittany spaniel. Almost afraid to hope for too much, I made an appointment with her for the next day.

From the moment I met this woman I knew there was something most unusual about her. I was amazed at her gentleness and at the depth of feeling she showed when she spoke. In the course of questioning her and listening to her life story, I became convinced that this was the right person for Penny. She thought so, too, and we began exchanging names, addresses, and phone numbers so we could arrange to turn Penny over.

When Penny's new owner handed her information to me, I was absolutely stunned. Her last name was Christmas! She saw the look on my face and she laughed. She pulled out her driver's license, saying, "I know, I get these reactions all the time. But that's my real name! Here, look." She went on to say, "Having a name like mine, I get to bring a lot of joy into people's lives."

But though she was used to the response she got from her name, I don't think she had ever thought of her name as a direct and literal answer to a prayer. I wasn't in any condition to explain; I could barely talk. My mind was racing a hundred miles a minute and trying to absorb how clearly and astonishingly my prayer had been answered. Surely God was laughing with both of us.

I gathered my thoughts enough to set a time to turn Penny over to her, and as she drove away, I realized that I had, indeed, been given a Christmas present in July!

Three good homes for three good dogs—and each home so perfect and such a direct answer to my prayer that I never again questioned the existence of divinity or my connection to Spirit. Though I had many interesting challenges in my life in the years that followed, that spiritual connection has never been severed. In the years I was blessed to know them, my dogs gave me many gifts, and the greatest gift was this: because of them, I would never again question the existence of God.

- - - - - - - - - - - - - - -

This chapter is entitled "Spirituality" and in it, I talk about living a life that is spiritually fulfilling because it is lived from a place of Spirit. *Webster's New World College Dictionary*, Third Edition, defines *spirituality* as "spiritual character, quality, or nature; the fact or state of being incorporeal."

The word *spirituality* comes from the root word *spiritual*, which means "of spirit or the soul as distinguished from the body or material matters." If we further break the word *spiritual* down to its root, *spirit*, we can discern a deeper meaning: "a divine animating influence or inspiration." I take the word *animating* to mean that Spirit influences and inspires in a way that manifests change in our lives.

I believe that we are divine beings, and that our purpose is to bring forth that divinity to give our lives meaning and fulfillment. Everything we see in our known Universe comes from Spirit. Everything—your best friend comes from Spirit, as does your worst enemy. Each brings gifts, lessons, and truths to our lives. When we can embrace the concept that every person, situation, and lesson we encounter emanates from Spirit and Spirit's love for us, then we truly begin to see the sacred in life and the extent of Spirit's affirming presence in our lives.

Life is a process into which Spirit brings events, challenges, and influences to help our consciousness evolve. I believe Spirit affects and scripts every aspect of our lives. Once our consciousness, our awareness, evolves to the point that we see Spirit's hand at work in our lives, we begin to recognize our own spiritual origin and the spiritual origin of others. Our evolution is the result of acknowledging that *our joys and our challenges are equal gifts.* We learn from both, evolving in our awareness and, in time, waking up to our own divinity.

The story I shared about my dogs and my prayer for them and how that prayer was answered illustrates how Spirit can move in our lives, often beyond our understanding and beyond our wildest hopes. It is just one of the many instances in my life that has served to affirm Spirit for me, and that has inspired me to write about Spirit. The power that answered my prayer and that continues to act in my life is not just accessible to me—it is accessible to you as well. My hope is that this story, and the other stories in this book, will trigger a connection for you, bringing to mind instances of Spirit moving in your own life and giving you the sense that there is a divine purpose in all that you experience. We are all part of an amazing story that is unfolding, and if we have the courage to follow our hearts and pay attention to the Divine, our lives take on a whole new perspective.

No matter what has occurred in your life—no matter what someone has done to you or for you, or whether you have experienced injustice or good fortune, joy or disappointment—you have the power to access your own divinity in any moment to bring you what you desire in life or help you through any dilemma. *This book is about that power* and the ways you can make a connection to it in the present moment to give purpose to your life and bring you the joy and affirmation you were meant to know.

It is a guide, a roadmap. I believe that, if you follow it, you will come to realize that you are not separate from Spirit and that you *are* Spirit. Then, living from your own divinity, you can create the world you desire, a world filled with love, joy, contentment, peace, compassion, and prosperity.

The choice is ours. Spirit meets us where are in our choice making and where we are in our consciousness. So envision what you desire, and

7

feel it with great passion; act on it with good intention, and by paying attention to the present, the world becomes your canvas, waiting for your paintbrush.

- - - - - - - - - - - - - - -

A friend suggested to me one day that I use the word "Divine" instead of "God" when I talk about spirituality. He felt the word God was reserved for religion, and that I was talking about something broader. My response was that no one has a patent on the word God. While I do use many names for God—Deity, Spirit, or Divine, for example—that does not diminish, in my eyes, my love for this Higher Power. Nor do I believe I am being disrespectful to organized religion, either by using the word God or by using other terms to represent our Higher Power. I believe we must allow each other to worship and love God in whatever way we feel appropriate. On this planet we have many names for God, but that does not in any way change how this power operates. God is!

My Thoughts—

"One God, One Law, One Element, and One far-off divine event, to which the whole creation moves."

—Alfred Lord Tennyson

9

For my desires to manifest, I must be able to envision them. Likewise, if I cannot envision something I desire, it cannot be available to me. How can I manifest what I desire? First, by knowing that *everything I desire is already in my consciousness*. Then, by envisioning what I want, knowing that it is possible for me to achieve what I envision. And finally, by using passion and longing to connect to that desire. I have the power to create my own reality; if I perceive that I am missing something in my life, I need only to be able to envision it and desire it. This is spirituality—realizing I am Spirit, that all I desire in life comes from Spirit, and that, by connecting with Spirit, all I desire in my life can be accessed *now*!

My Thoughts—

"God is a sea of infinite substance."

—St. John of Damascus

When I am contemplating choices in my life, I know the true path I should take resides with my Higher Self, which is my divinity. Though my Higher Self knows, intuitively, the path I should take, my conscious mind insists on rationalizing my decisions, creating a "pro and con" list, and emphasizing the negative. I am learning to listen to my intuitive Higher Self. I want my choice making to evolve until, in each moment, I am guided and directed by my divinity. My challenge in evolving is to quiet my conscious mind so that I can recognize Spirit directing me. I know that my own mind is the only thing that separates me from Spirit, causing me to listen to the wrong advice or to give all my attention to the negative aspect of the choice I'm facing. How can I quiet my mind and hear the message my Higher Self is sending?

My Thoughts—

"Know thyself."

—Proverb

I have discovered that there is no hard and fast rule by which to access divinity. Each person is unique. Because divinity comes from within, rather than through external forces such as wealth, career, or life partner, each person's means of accessing divinity is unique as well. Our ability to get in touch with divinity is not learned overnight, but rather is a process. We must first be willing to look within and search for our divine connection. Then we learn to align our choice making from that connection. Finally, we become able to share that connection with people and connect to the things that are important to us. At that point, we begin to attract the things to our lives that we really desire.

My Thoughts—

"My greatest desire is that I may perceive the God whom I find everywhere in the external world, in like manner also within and inside myself."

—Johannes Kepler

When I focus on my bank account, the number of clients I am attracting, the stock market, or whether my children think I am a good father, I am totally externalized in my perspective. I am concentrating on the effects of the influences in my life instead of the causes, and so am not accessing the divinity within me. To what elements of my life have I given too much attention? What external things in my life distract me from the power of the divinity within and my divine connection?

My Thoughts—

"All that you do makes
it impossible for what
already is there to
express itself."

—U. G. Krishnamurti

I watched a video this morning and its main theme was, "Until I can believe it, I will not see it." Later in the day I revisited a company for which I had served as a consultant several years ago. My experience with this company had convinced me that, in spite of my best efforts, its managers would never be able to work together in a supportive, productive way. On becoming reacquainted with them, I was surprised to find they were doing a much better job of interfacing with each other and were now open to learning how to improve their working relationships. I didn't know what caused the improvement and found myself wondering whether the people in the company might have had the desire, and ability, to work together before, and whether it might have been my own attitude about them that held them back. I know it is possible my perceptions of them had manifested in reality; likewise, I know that changing my belief about the company and seeing its progress might have made that possibility a reality.

My Thoughts—

"Rub your eyes and be
awake."

—Mikhail Naimy

The video I referred to in the previous passage carried a valuable lesson: "Until I believe it, I will not see it." I believe this insight is the key to understanding a vital point about Spirit: that whatever we need in our lives, Spirit has already provided it. We just have to believe it. Again and again, my research and revelations from my own life remind me that God's resources, and my own, are unlimited. The *only* limitations in our lives are those which we impose on ourselves with our thoughts and belief systems—the Divine lacks for nothing. When our worldview evolves enough to understand that, we finally will see the power of God in our lives and understand that there is no separation between God and ourselves.

My Thoughts—

"God is the East and
the West, and wherever
ye turn, there is God's
face."

—St. John of Damascus

I believe the "kingdom of heaven" is here, now, if we choose to believe it and see it. Likewise, I think some people create their own personal "hell" here on earth, through the choices they make. We are all in the process of becoming, and instead of judging a person or judging their lifestyle, I choose instead to imagine what other choices a person might make that would lead to a more positive outcome. I then interact with this person from this perspective of possibility, rather than from a judgmental perspective. Making choices and treating people with love, compassion, and generosity lets me bring the kingdom of heaven into the present moment for myself and for an individual. What positive and constructive choices did I make in my interactions with others today?

My Thoughts—

"The divine nature, free and perfect and blissful, must be manifested in the individual in order that it may manifest in the world."

—The Shivapuri Baba

Spirit is all-knowing, and because we are Spirit, we are all-knowing as well. We must have the courage to embrace this reality. We must be willing to see the sacred in life. There is no separation between Spirit and ourselves—there is only the One. What fears keep me from embracing this truth?

My Thoughts—

"There is one God; and there is none other than He."

—Mark 12:32

17

David D. Dameron

The laws of the spiritual world and the material world are one and the same. I found myself being judged one day by someone who based their judgment of me on something I believed was untrue. On looking closely at the situation, I realized that I had been responsible in the past for judging this person based on some of his choices. I believe in the saying, "What goes around, comes around"! The energy we send out returns to us; the outside world is a reflection of our inside world. Who in my life have I judged and what are these people showing me about myself?

My Thoughts—

"Why do you want to open the outside door when there is an inside door? Everything is within."

—Yogaswami

A well-known tenet of theology is the saying, "As you sow, so shall you reap." The law of return is a spiritual law well worth embracing. Incorporate it into your life; demonstrate it in your thoughts, words, and actions. Know that whatever we send out returns to us. What thoughts and energy do I want to send out? What words do I want to speak? What actions can I take to create a positive effect in people's lives and, in return, in my own life?

My Thoughts—

"The spiritual is not to be separated from the material, nor the wonderful from the ordinary."

—Alan Watts

I met God today. That's right, you heard me! I met God today in the form of an idea. That idea was the inspiration to write this book. The thought came to me that this book could further the ideas put forth in my first book. When I felt the excitement behind this idea, I knew I was being given direction and inspiration from my divinity. In what other ways have I met God? In what ways does God speak to me?

My Thoughts—

"We are co-creators with God, not puppets on a string waiting for something to happen."

—Leo Booth

Last night I spoke with my wife, Susan, about some fears I had about our future and about my choice to embrace a belief in abundance. I had let all of my clients go to concentrate on writing this book. In the past, I would have finished the book and then begun an intensive period of marketing and trying to reach my financial goals. But I choose to live my life differently today. The reality is that I do not want to continue approaching my life as a billing statement. I have chosen to manifest abundance and prosperity in my life, not through initial plans and efforts, but by *going to the source from which all things spring*: my divinity. How am I connecting with my source on a daily basis to manifest abundance in my life?

My Thoughts—

"Man thinks,
God directs."

—Alcuin, *Epistles*

21

I decided today that if what we send out returns to us, I want to put only positive energy out into the world, through both what I say and what I think. I want to remember that all spoken words and thoughts are recorded in Spirit, and that what I send out returns to me by law. It's important to me to rid myself and my thoughts of judgments, criticisms, and negativity. I'm finding it isn't easy to change the habits of a lifetime and become vigilant with my words and thoughts! How can I make this change a reality in my life?

My Thoughts—

"There is one divine mind which keeps the Universe in order and one providence which governs it."

—Plutarch

Metaphysics explains the energy behind the law of return. According to *Webster's New World Dictionary*, *metaphysics* is "the branch of philosophy that deals with first principles and seeks to explain the nature of being or reality and the origin and structure of the Universe." Metaphysical philosophy teaches that energy follows thought. This is how Spirit works. Whatever we impress upon Spirit in our words, thoughts, feelings, and actions is what Spirit returns to us. Spirit mirrors our thoughts back to us, whether the thought was positive or negative. I must embrace the moment and be totally conscious of my actions, realizing that I am responsible for what I attract in my life, whether that be good things or challenges that serve as lessons. What did I learn today about my thoughts and choice making?

My Thoughts—

"I have (come) to the heartfelt realization that spirituality is simply the part of me that longs for fulfillment."

—Carol Osborn

If you want to gauge how you are doing spiritually, look at your external world. Take a look at your career: Are you inspired and motivated by your work? Do you have loving relationships in your life? Are you in good health? Are you stable financially? Are you fulfilled? Do you have peace of mind? The world is a mirror of our spirit and the choices we make. If you perceive yourself to be lacking in any of these ways, then explore your relationship with Spirit in these areas and examine what your beliefs and actions have been. In what areas of my life would I like to improve? What beliefs in these areas would I like to change? How do I go about making changes in my beliefs? Perhaps I can pattern the changes based on areas in my life that I already find fulfilling!

My Thoughts—

"All I have seen teaches me to trust the creator for all I have not seen."

—Ralph Waldo Emerson

Once your connection with Spirit becomes part of your life, the smallest things can convey powerful messages. While putting a plug into a wall socket today, I realized how powerful it is to be "plugged in" to my relationship with God. When I am feeling connected to my spirit, I'm connected to the power that keeps my life in balance. Likewise, when I am anxious and moody, I know I have pulled the plug from the wall. (God would never pull the plug out!) I know, in these moments, I need only plug back into the source to get reconnected. What actions can I take to stay connected with Spirit? How can Spirit become more present in my life in this very moment? What can I do to better see the sacred in all of life?

My Thoughts—

"Into thy hands I commend my spirit."

—Luke 23:46

Regardless of what is occurring in your life, you are truly never alone in your journey. When you are confused, despairing, or afraid, know that you have both visible and invisible helpers to assist you. You need only invite these angels into your life and ask for their help. The answer to your prayer may come in unexpected ways—from a person on a street corner or through a voice you hear only in your mind. Be open to hearing the angels' response and pay attention to their guidance. In this moment, right now, ask yourself, "Am I open to receiving help? Do I believe that help is available to me whenever I ask?" Remember to ask and you shall receive!

My Thoughts—

"The sole purpose of this human life is nothing but the realization of God. Meditate on Him with as much reverence and love as you can."

—The Shivapuri Baba

There is a religious saying, "As above, so below." In the introduction to this book I wrote of my marriage to Susan. That marriage is a mirror of a deeper marriage—the union between David (or Susan) and Spirit. Both are sacred marriages. Everything that I do in the physical, external world is a mirror of my presence in the spiritual world. I may plant a seed in my garden; likewise, I may plant a seed with Spirit, asking for something I deeply desire. In what other areas of my life does my external, objective world reflect my inner, spiritual world?

My Thoughts—

"We do not walk to God with the feet of our body, nor would wings, if we had them, carry us to Him, but we go to Him, by the affections of our soul."

—St. Augustine

CHAPTER TWO:

THE PRESENT

"If it is the quality of your consciousness at this moment that determines the future, then what is it that determines the quality of your consciousness? Your degree of presence."

—Eckhart Tolle, *The Power of Now*

How many times have you come home tired from a long day's work just wanting to sit down and relax, only to find someone wants you to do something for them? How does it feel when unexpected interruptions arise, pulling you in a new and unappealing direction? Have you ever been delayed in traffic when you really needed to reach your destination quickly? Put aside the frustration these situations create and consider this: these struggles against where we are, as compared to where we want to be, have the added downside of taking us out of the present moment.

I'm going to tell you the story of a good friend of mine who found herself in such a frustrating situation and, from it, learned the power of being present in the moment. Cherie is a self-employed businesswoman, who markets and counsels her clients on the use of high-grade essential oils. These are aromatic, volatile liquids that have been used for centuries for a number of purposes, from religious rituals to the treatment of illnesses and other physical and spiritual needs. Cherie had been traveling by plane from her hometown in Minnesota to a conference in Baltimore, Maryland. It had been a grueling week of travel for her already, and she was tired and very much looking forward to sleeping on the flight.

She boarded her plane and, as it took off, Cherie settled back in her seat and started to doze off. Just minutes later the flight attendant came over the PA system and asked if there was a medical professional on board, as one of the passengers, a woman who was seven months pregnant, had gone into labor.

Cherie knew that a woman who was seven months pregnant could go into labor as a result of the changes in air pressure on airline flights. Hearing the announcement, she thought to herself, "Oh Lord, not me. I am so tired." But, being the person she is, and knowing her purpose, Cherie focused on her heart and asked, "Is this mine to do?" The answer she heard did not surprise her. The voice inside her replied, "And you needed to ask?"

So Cherie pushed the call button, and when flight attendant came, Cherie told the attendant, "I am not a medical professional, but I am trained in the proper use of therapeutic-grade essential oils, and they have been proven to stop early labor." The flight attendant politely responded that there was a nurse practitioner on board who was seeing to the pregnant woman, and they would come and get Cherie if they needed her. So Cherie went back to sleep thinking that maybe all she had needed to do was just respond to her inner voice. Apparently, she was going to be allowed to get some sleep after all.

A few minutes later Cherie was awakened by the flight attendant, tapping on her shoulder. "We need you," said the flight attendant. So Cherie gathered her oils and went to the back of the plane, where the pregnant woman was lying on the floor.

She found the nurse practitioner doing her best to help the woman. But Cherie noticed that the woman was not only in labor—she was vomiting and having extreme anxiety attacks. The flight attendant whispered in Cherie's ear, "Can you do something?" Cherie responded that she could.

Suddenly, a most peculiar thing happened. The flight attendant told the nurse practitioner, "You're out, she's in," referring to Cherie. Kneeling down to the woman in labor, Cherie tried to talk to the woman, but there was no response. The pregnant woman was completely overwhelmed with anxiety, pain, and terror.

Cherie grabbed a bottle of lavender oil out of her purse, put some in her hand, and rubbed it over the woman's stomach. She held her hand on the woman's stomach and silently prayed. In less than five minutes, the woman opened her eyes very wide, looked at Cherie and said, "They've stopped. My contractions have stopped!" Gratefully, the woman asked Cherie who she was, and Cherie responded, "I'm Cherie. I'm here to help you."

Cherie continued to care for the pregnant woman, using various oils to treat her vomiting, nausea, and anxiety. Slowly, the woman stabilized. As the plane approached Baltimore, Cherie stayed close to her.

When the plane landed, the EMTs boarded and told Cherie they would take over. The flight attendant requested that Cherie stay until everyone else had departed from the airplane. Cherie gathered her things and filed out behind the last passenger and found the captain waiting to greet her. He took her hand and said, "Thank you." Cherie responded, "You're welcome," and started to leave.

Cherie then realized that the captain would not let go of her hand as he thanked her again. "I was happy to help," Cherie said. "It's part of my job. Anyone who could have helped would have done the same thing."

But the captain's response surprised Cherie. "You don't have any idea what was going on before and during your intervention, do you?" he asked.

"I guess not," Cherie replied.

The captain then told her that when the pregnant woman went into labor, he had contacted a medical team on the ground. The team had determined that the plane would have to make an emergency landing, and the pilot had been in the process of looking for an airport with a runway long enough to land the plane safely. The pilot had stayed on the radio with the medical team. What Cherie did not know was that the flight attendant who had quizzed her on what she was using had also been communicating with the medical team.

The attendant had described what Cherie was doing and described, as well, how quickly the pregnant woman responded. The medical team conferred and, even though they could not quite understand the nature of the treatment, they told the flight attendant to let Cherie continue. "Because of what you did, that mother has a chance to carry her child to term. And we avoided making an emergency landing, and got all the people on this plane to Baltimore after all!"

Cherie departed the plane with a warm feeling in her heart. She had listened to her guiding voice, and, in spite of the stress of the situation, had chosen to share her gift. In spite of her fatigue and in spite of all the activity going on around her, Cherie stayed in the moment, focusing on her role as a healer. Because she did, she may have saved a woman's life and the life of an unborn child.

- - - - - - - - - - - - - -

When I heard this story, I thought to myself, "What a great story of being present and in the moment." This chapter is about the present and the power of staying in the present. How many times during our day do we let our minds wander to something that has happened in the past or something we are anticipating in the future instead of focusing on the here and now?

The reality is that the only time that truly exists is the *now*. Really think about this point. What happened a few minutes ago is only a memory. What could happen has not yet occurred. It follows that there is only *this* moment.

Each and every moment brings another opportunity to be present. Being present in the moment is one of the things I try to help my clients learn. I tell them, "When you desire something in your life, the key is to pay attention to what is happening around you and inside you, each moment. When you need help or are searching for an answer, just be present, listen, and be cognizant of what you are thinking or what is happening internally for you. The answer is in the *now*."

The world we live in is moving at such a rapid pace that it is very easy to lose our focus. Information reaches us at lightning speed, whether by cell phone, pager, e-mail, or fax. When we lose our focus, we lose the power of our concentration, and our thoughts scatter in all directions.

Every chapter in this book is ultimately about the power of staying present in the moment. The *now* is a sacred place where we find our spirit and decide what choices we will make, what thoughts will hold our focus.

The truth is that peace, joy, love, contentment, and guidance are all waiting for us in the moment. From the minute you open your eyes in the morning to the moment you fall asleep at night (and even in your dreams!), there are no ordinary moments. In each and every moment, you are either moving toward your potential or you are moving away from your divinity. Every experience is teaching you on a moment-by-moment basis.

Turn from the past, let go of the future, and know that the present is all there is. The present is, indeed, a present. It is the sacred moment that holds our divinity, the place where we can realize that our lives are a reflection of the choices we make and the things we choose to honor with our attention, moment by moment. You have the power to choose to live in this sacred place, in the midst of all that is sacred in life.

- - - - - - - - - - - - - -

We choose *how* we experience life in each moment. We have a choice as to how we will respond to each thought or occurrence. For that reason, I need to be a "gatekeeper" to my thoughts and reactions. I need to ask myself whether my thought or reaction is based in love and understanding, or whether is it rooted in fear or anxiety. I know that positive thoughts and reactions return positive things to me and to my life. I have a choice in each moment—I choose my thoughts and reactions carefully to bring good things into my life.

My Thoughts—

"When the mind is not in harmony, this divine communion is hard to attain; but the man whose mind is in harmony attains it, if he knows and if he strives."

—The *Bhagavad-Gita*

David D. Dameron

I control my thoughts; my thoughts do not control me. I know that what I send out returns to me (like in the saying, "What goes around comes around"), so it is prudent for me to pay attention to what I am thinking and what I am saying. Being mindful of our thoughts, words, and actions is a tremendous responsibility that, as divine beings, we can choose to accept. The world mirrors our thoughts and our words, reflecting them and their energy back to us. I need to be mindful in each moment of my thoughts and words, and mindful of what I am honoring with my attention.

My Thoughts—

"I have already realized that all beings and all phenomena are of one's own mind. The mind itself is a transparency of voidness."

—Milarepa

How do we make our ideas manifest in our lives? If, for example, I desire a fulfilling and well-paying job, how can I go about attracting it? We attract what we desire in life by imagining what we want, feeling what we want with great passion, and then acting on our idea. In order to accomplish our dreams and ideas, we bring our focus into the present moment. We must actually imagine what we desire as actually already having been given to us. We must fully embrace in our mind and heart what we desire in the "now." What keeps me from losing my focus when I am trying to imagine my desire? How can I control my mind, keep it from wandering, and learn how to stay present in the moment?

My Thoughts—

"The future is purchased
by the present."

—Samuel Johnson

David D. Dameron

Meditation is a wonderfully useful tool that teaches us to stay present in the moment. Although there are many forms of meditation, the technique I use is very simple. I either sit in a chair, with my spine straight, or I sit cross-legged on the floor, and I close my eyes. I begin concentrating on my breath, breathing deeply and slowly, and expanding the area around my stomach with each breath. I concentrate on my breath. As thoughts come into my mind, I shift my focus back to my breath. I do this for about ten minutes before I begin my workday. I feel much more centered and focused in the moment when my day has included meditation.

My Thoughts—

"What is beyond the mind has no boundary; in it, our senses end."

—Mira Bai

One of the ways I practice my ability to be present is to spend as much time in nature as possible. I look for the beauty in nature in my own backyard or in a nearby park. I watch the insects and the animals and I give close attention to the scenery around me, consciously focusing on the beauty in things. This practice of observing nature has taught me that I can be present anywhere I am. I find when I make a practice of observing nature, it becomes much easier to remain focused and in the present moment, throughout my day. One of the many advantages to this practice is that my ability to be present in the moment makes me a better listener. As I have developed this skill, my friends and clients have told me that they feel I am really listening to them—and I am!

My Thoughts—

"Gather ye rosebuds while ye may, old time is still-a-flying; and this same flower that smiles today tomorrow will be dying."

—Robert Herrick

David D. Dameron

Based on my research and my direct experience of life, I have come to two conclusions: first, that everything in the Universe is Spirit; and second, that everything is energy. When I pay attention to things around me while holding this focus, I feel connected to life and see the sacred in life. In seeing everything—those things we might consider positive and things we might consider negative—as an expression of Spirit and energy, I sense the energy of my own mind and my connection to all I see. Through that connection, the world around me becomes beautiful, in all its aspects. Because what I send out returns to me, the beauty I send out is reflected back to me. Likewise, if I see all of life as divine, then the Divine is reflected back to me. This truth is one of the secrets to living a spiritually fulfilling life.

My Thoughts—

"Our essence of mind is intrinsically pure; all things are only its manifestations, and good and evil deeds are only the result of good thoughts and evil thoughts respectively."

—Wei Lang

Yesterday, while I was meditating, I found myself contemplating a challenge I had attracted to myself. Though in my mind I knew that this challenge was a gift and a manifestation of Spirit in my life, I could not see anything to be gained from my struggle with it, and I found myself asking, "Where *is* God in this situation?" The gentle answer that came back to me was, "I am here." Suddenly, the situation was no longer about a difficult challenge; it was about the presence of God. I realized that God had always been with me. I knew in my heart—not just in my mind—that with God present in all things, my challenge was truly a positive force. Then I truly knew, in my heart, that regardless of whether I could see the positive aspects or not, this situation was an opportunity and a gift.

My Thoughts—

"If the chimney is full of
smoke, how can the light
be seen? If the mind is
full of dirt, how can the
soul shine?"

—Yogaswami

41

David D. Dameron

I once heard one of my spiritual teachers tell a group of workshop attendees that he was a man without a past. His point was that life is a "do over." Whatever has occurred in the past is only a memory. The future will be forged only by how we handle our thinking and actions in the present. What past memories do I need to release, and how can I better focus on the present?

My Thoughts—

"Today is the best preparation we have for what tomorrow may bring."

—Anonymous

42

During my meditation this morning, I realized there are two areas of my meditation practice that I would like to improve. First, I want to become adept at turning off my brain, both when I'm meditating and when I am not. I tend to think about what I need to do or a problem I am working through, instead of staying in the present moment and trusting that Spirit will work things out for the best. Second, I need to concentrate on the *source* of what I desire (my divinity), instead of focusing on *outcomes*. When I am in need of something, my focus tends to dwell on the need itself instead of on the source of good outcomes—my divinity. God is the source of endless abundance, and through Spirit, all outcomes far exceed my desires and needs.

My Thoughts—

"Practice and thought might gradually forge many an art."

—Virgil

David D. Dameron

As I said in my first book (and in this one), the purpose of our humanity is to allow divinity to unfold in us through our choice making. That said, it's important to step out of the idea that we are unfolding and evolving and know that, in every moment, we are—already—an aspect of the Divine. Everything I desire has already been provided for me in this moment. Although things often take time to manifest on this physical plane, we must realize that there is no lack, in ourselves or in the world, when seen in the light of God's abundance.

My Thoughts—

"I don't need to do anything with the self, I don't need to improve it or make it good or sacrifice it or crucify it—I don't need to do anything because it isn't even there...."

—Joanna Macy

My wife designs and makes these wonderful quilts that I firmly believe will bring her worldwide recognition one day. I asked her once what she thinks about when she is working on her quilts. She answered, "When I sew, I sew." A simple answer, and a simple approach, but what a remarkable state of mind her response represents. I realized that, when I am in the present moment, all things are immediate and clear. When I eat, I eat. When I teach, I teach. When I talk to my children, I talk to my children. The way my wife approaches her quilting wonderfully illustrates the power of being present in the moment.

My Thoughts—

"No time like the present."

—Proverb

I am changing my approach to attracting new business clients. Instead of worrying about how I can make new business opportunities come to me, I am learning how to go to Spirit in the moment and turn my future business opportunities over to my internal marketing director. That director's voice keeps saying, "Don't pursue. Live in the moment." This approach doesn't mean I just sit in my house, waiting for something to happen. I have to do my part. Each day, I pay attention to the various people I meet—they often seem to have been placed in my path to provide business opportunity. While I cannot always explain how this attraction works, I can tell you it does work and happens on a consistent basis. What I have realized is that my role is to provide the desire and to remain in touch with Spirit; God then handles the "hows" and makes things happen. In what other areas of my life can I turn my desires over to Spirit?

My Thoughts—

"What is love? 'Tis not hereafter; Present mirth hath present laughter ... What's to come is still unsure. In delay, there lies no plenty; Then come kiss me, sweet and twenty; Youth's a stuff will not endure."

—William Shakespeare

Life is about cycles. Our lives will feature times of easy rhythms and times when we have challenging rhythms. How intensely I feel these rhythms is a result of my attitude and how I perceive my life's changes. When I am present in the moment, I understand consciously what cycle I am experiencing. If I perceive the rhythm as challenging, I can keep it from lasting too long by not becoming obsessed with it and giving it negative energy. Likewise, when I am focused and in the moment during a positive rhythm, I can use that energy to remain energized and motivated. I discovered this key factor: *what I give my attention to returns to me.* By giving energy to positive rhythms, that energy returns; by not giving energy to negative rhythms, I shorten and lessen their impact. The choice is mine! I choose to emphasize the positive.

My Thoughts—

"There is nothing either good or bad but thinking makes it so."

—William Shakespeare

David D. Dameron

I played golf with some of my clients today. Instead of thinking about how poorly I played last week, I decided to enjoy the scenery and concentrate on each and every shot. I stayed in the moment, not thinking about the shot I'd just taken or a tough hole that lay ahead. The result was that I shot the best round in my life! Even when I hit a bad shot, I managed to put it out of my mind and stay in the moment. My approach turned each shot into a new opportunity. I realized how many areas of my life—driving, eating, speaking with people, observing, listening, playing the piano, working in the garden—would be improved if I could stay in the moment and be fully present.

My Thoughts—

"The best day of my life ... what actually happened was something absurdly simple and unspectacular: just for the moment I stopped thinking. Reason and Imagination and all mental chatter died down."

—Douglas Harding

While working in the yard today, I realized I had way too much mind traffic going on. In my mind, I was in an endless loop of negative self-talk. I realized that in this state of being, unfocused and scattered in my thoughts, I was not listening to my guidance. I realized that for some time, my guidance had been trying to tell me something, but all the mind chatter I had going on kept me from hearing. I was beginning to focus my mind on that inner voice when I found out exactly what it had been trying to convey—I put my hand into a fire ant hill. Talk about coming into the moment—the pain really did that for me! When I reflected about this episode, I asked myself, "How can I be more present in what I am doing? How can I learn to better recognize my inner guidance?"

My Thoughts—

"Where are the thoughts located? They are not in the brain. Thoughts are not manufactured by the brain. It is, rather, that the brain is like an antenna, picking up thoughts on a common wavelength, a common thought-sphere."

—Krisnamurti

Today, my wife and I were comparing the scars we've accumulated from not being in the moment. I pointed out several bumps and scars on my legs and my head where I had walked into tables or bumped my knee over the years, while not paying attention. She was laughing at the evidence of my inadequacy, until I pointed out similar scars on her legs, acquired through a similar lack of attention. We ended up laughing at each other. That led us to talk about other areas of our lives where we are sometimes unfocused—like letting our minds wander when we are driving. Not only does such a lack of focus put us out of touch with Spirit, it can be downright dangerous. We began talking about ways we can be more focused and present in whatever we are doing.

My Thoughts—

"Happy the man who could search out the causes of things."

—Virgil

I often talk about listening to my little voice. Once a friend asked me just who I thought my little voice was. Without hesitation, I answered, "My spiritual helpers." I have learned over the years that when I quiet my mind and focus on the present, I can ask a question, and then get my answer by listening to the first thing that comes into my head. Sometimes the answer is in words; often it is just a feeling. If you practice this as I do, you will learn to hear your own little voice—or voices! We are not alone. But to make good use of the voice and its responses, it is vital to recognize the difference between the voice of your spirit and the voices of judgment, criticism, and self-condemnation.

My Thoughts—

"The universe is transformation; our life is what our thoughts make it."

—Marcus Aurelius

Today gave me a great opportunity to learn how better to be present. My mother-in-law had passed away, and my wife's entire family had gathered to pay their respects. As with many families, there are some members of my wife's family who often have problems with other members, and as the day progressed, there was some family drama. Instead of being pulled into some of the family disputes, I remained calm and remembered why we had come: to pay our respects to my wife's mother. I really discovered today how I can be in the middle of something challenging and remain centered emotionally by just being present in the moment and keeping myself unattached to events, outcomes, or personalities.

My Thoughts—

"Carpe Diem."
("Seize the day.")

—Horace

Worry, anxiety, fear, and insecurities all take me out of the moment. When I am in these states, I am usually projecting into the future, worried about something that has not even happened. To regain my composure, all I need to do is bring my focus into the present. The energy I put out returns to me. Consequently, if my future desires are affected by my choices and mindsets in the moment, I need to switch my thoughts to what I desire in the present and not sabotage them with fearful thinking. From my years of consulting with my clients and working on my own personal issues, I have come to believe that fear is the single most destructive emotion, with an incredible power to impact our lives. What fears do I allow to distract me from being present in the moment?

My Thoughts—

"Believe that each day that has dawned is your last. Some hour to which you have not been looking forward will prove lovely."

—Horace

I teach my clients that to develop an *anchor list* to bring their focus back to the present when they are experiencing negative thoughts or feelings. An anchor list is a list of memories that bring you pleasure or make you laugh, every time you think of them. When I think of certain things my wife and I have done together, my mind and emotions respond positively. When I think of my children and fun things we have done together, those images create positive feelings within me. When I think of the music of Brian Wilson, my spirit just soars. What things can you think of that bring you positive feelings and improve your attitude when you are feeling negative?

My Thoughts—

"Moments of true consciousness, unconditioned by the self, are usually fleeting but indelible. We always remember them. They remain to us as moments out of time."

—Anne Bancroft

In each moment, I choose to allow my beliefs and attitudes to be changed to let me more fully realize the divine hand at work in my life. I am an aspect of God; therefore, I have no need to worry about anything. When I stay present and focused on the all-sufficiency of Spirit, it brings to me whatever I desire in life. When I see the sacred in life, then I bring forth my own divinity. I thank God for the present!

My Thoughts—

"For everything that lives is holy, life delights in life."

—William Blake

CHAPTER THREE:

INTUITION

"Intuition is perception beyond the physical senses that is meant to assist you. It is that sensory system which operates without data from the five senses. Your intuitional system is part of your incarnation."

—Gary Zukav, *The Seat of the Soul*

Premonitions. Hunches. The feeling that comes over you when your hair stands up on the back of your neck. All of these things are part of the gift of intuition, and can save or direct our lives if we are paying attention. I know this for a fact, as my intuition saved my life in the summer of 1968.

I was traveling through Europe with seven of my high school friends and my foreign language teacher. We were bicycling through several countries and traveling by train through others. Mid-July found us in Paris to celebrate Bastille Day, which is the equivalent of our July 4th holiday here in the United States.

On Bastille Day, Paris closes many of its streets to motor traffic, and people congregate and participate in a celebration similar to Mardi Gras that lasts all day long and into the night. In this particular year, though the atmosphere was one of celebration, there was an underlying tension in the city as well. There had been a number of student demonstrations in Paris in the past weeks. The news had been full of clashes between police and students over government policies.

The group I was with was aware of the hostilities, but we had been looking forward to the evening's festivities, and we convinced ourselves that, if we were cautious, we could participate safely. We were wrong. By the end of the evening, we would realize that the situation, combined with our lack of caution, had put all of our lives in serious danger.

We began our evening by walking from our hotel to a cozy, French bistro for dinner. When we walked out of the restaurant, we found ourselves on a street corner among several groups of people who had begun singing and dancing. I was watching the people when I spotted a group of gendarmes, or French policeman, approaching.

On the surface, nothing looked wrong; the policemen appeared casual, on a routine patrol. But in an instant, my intuition told me the approaching encounter would not be casual at all. I remember that the hair on the back of my neck stood up and a loud voice inside my head said, *"Run!"*

I did not think. I did not reason. I did not even have the time to turn to my friends and tell them what I was going to do. In an instant, without quite knowing why, I took off running down an intersecting street. I glanced back to see my friends looking after me in amazement. I was in motion; but they were still, almost in a state of suspended animation.

Then I saw the patrolling gendarmes reach the crowd and turn to face them, their shields and their nightsticks raised as they encircled everyone on the street corner and began to beat them without mercy. Part of me wanted to go back to help my friends; a more realistic part of me told me told me I was vastly outnumbered and to keep running and seek help.

I saw another group of gendarmes gathered on a street corner. I ran up to them, telling them my friends were in trouble and pleading with them to help me. One of the gendarmes responded by hitting me in the back with his nightstick and telling me to move along.

I was exhausted, horrified, and in shock, and my mind was racing a hundred miles an hour as I desperately tried to think of what I should do or where I could go. I finally decided to circle around and return to the square.

I felt like I was in a motion picture, playing out a role: *an American trapped in Paris, separated from his friends, tries to avoid capture as he traverses the backstreets of the city.* But the situation was real, as the pain in my back where the nightstick had struck reminded me.

I finally made it back to the square and found it in absolute chaos. People were screaming; others were lying motionless on the concrete with blood all over their clothes. I was shaking with fear for my own safety and for the well-being of my friends.

As I sat down at a corner café to avoid the chaos, I saw some of my friends walking cautiously down the street. Relieved, I called to them and motioned them over to where I was sitting. It was a shock to see them; each of them had various bumps, bruises, and bloodstains from having been beaten. They sat down at my table, exhausted, and my friends in their bloodstained shirts and I tried to get past our panic and figure out how to reconnect with the rest of our group.

But before we could form a plan, the chaos escalated again. The café was struck with tear gas, and within seconds I found myself stumbling out into the street, unable to see and coughing violently from the gas. My friends and I managed to stay together, and about a block or so away, I saw two gendarmes standing by a police van. My instinct guided me again. On seeing them, I knew immediately, without knowing how, that they would help us.

We told them we were American tourists. They told us how to get back to our hotel and gave us a route that would not take us near the student rioters. As we crept down the Paris backstreets to our hotel, we caught glimpses of students clashing with the police and heard the sounds of the confrontation.

When we arrived at our hotel, we found the rest of our group had gotten there earlier and were waiting for us with their own tales of terror. They had called the American embassy to explain our predicament. That message had been conveyed to the French police, and word had been passed on to a command post on the streets to be on the lookout for us. The two gendarmes who helped us had recognized us from that message.

Our teacher called our parents to update them on the situation, and our parents and teacher decided our trip should continue. We left Paris the next day without further incident. But I still reflect from time to time on the voice that spoke to me so strongly and guided me through this harrowing experience.

- - - - - - - - - - - - - - -

As human beings, we take in information through our five senses: sight, touch, smell, taste, and hearing. We can reflect on this information and make choices. As children, we were taught about these five senses; but there is another source of information available to us and another faculty we can use to make decisions. That faculty is our "sixth sense," our intuition.

Unlike the other senses, intuition is an inner faculty, and one that does not always rely on outside information to form a conclusion. Our intuitive natures are a spiritual antenna; they serve to connect us directly with our divinity, our Higher Selves.

This intuitive faculty never fails us. It gives us a direct line to Spirit, functioning like a phone on which, in any moment, we can call God and ask what we should do.

Should I turn left or right going down this street? Should I do business with this person? Something does not feel right with my child. I know who is calling on that ringing telephone! All of these are examples of how our intuitive capabilities operate.

I have no doubts that my intuition saved me from serious injury that evening. I believe that my intuitive nature told me which street to run down and how to get to the café. I believe my intuition told me to trust the two gendarmes who told us how to get back to our hotel. It was the voice of the sacred in my life, protecting me and guiding me.

If you want to understand how God communicates with you and how you can begin to see the sacred in life, then become cognizant of how your intuition works. Our intuition operates totally in present time, and can advise us if we pay attention to it. How can we best access the information intuition provides? Ask Spirit a question; then follow your first reaction. Think of your intuition as your silent partner who travels with you wherever you go. It is comforting to know that we are not alone!

- - - - - - - - - - - - - - -

David D. Dameron

When we function in the intuitive realm, we are drawing conclusions through our feeling mode and receiving impressions from some mysterious source. What is this source? Could it be God? Could it be our spiritual helpers? Am I willing to trust this source? When functioning in the intuitive realm, I try to remain in the moment, because the intuitive realm is not about the past or the future. It really is about what is happening now—this very moment.

My Thoughts—

"Do not waste time in idle speculation or thinking but come within for quiet contemplation with the Master of your soul."

—Eva Bell Werber

In my journals I often speak about listening to my "little voice." Spiritual texts refer to the "little voice" as a "still, small voice." Often, it isn't intrusive; I have to make a bit of an effort to hear it. Be willing to follow your own voice and your hunches. Spend time recognizing what your "little voice" sounds like. The "little voice" is your intuitive guide and can provide another way for you to communicate with your divine spirit. What does my little voice sound like? What does it feel like? What is my "little voice" telling me? When I look back on what it told me, and what happened subsequently, how accurately had I heard what my voice was telling me?

My Thoughts—

"To love is to listen."

—Thich Nhat Hanh

David D. Dameron

I access my intuitive voice for all kinds of issues, large and small. Today I should have listened to my intuition. I went to a hardware store to buy an atomic alarm clock. The clocks came in different colors, and I first chose the blue one. As I noticed the clerk taking the blue alarm clock out of the cabinet, my eyes fell on a purple-colored clock. Something told me the purple clock was the one I should buy instead, but I said nothing. As it turned out, when I got home and plugged the blue clock in, it didn't work; I had to take it back and exchange it. I got the purple one, and it worked perfectly! In what other situations should I have listened to my intuition?

My Thoughts—

"A loud voice cannot compete with a clear voice, even if it's a whisper."

—Barry Neil Kaufman

One way I work on developing my intuition is to work with a deck of playing cards. With the cards face down, I try to intuit whether the next card is red or black. Then I try to predict what suit the card will be. I then try to guess the face value of the card *and* its suit, which is really hard to do accurately. I have found that when I take a breath, relax, and focus on the present, my success rate improves. Practicing relaxation, breathing, and focusing helps develop my intuitive faculty and affirms for me my ability to contact my intuitive voice.

My Thoughts—

"Believe that you are more, that you contain an inner self, a true self than can emerge only if you give it attention."

—Jean Houston

David D. Dameron

In meditation today, the message was given to me that I should learn to trust my intuition more often. When I asked how I could enhance my intuitive listening, the answer came back to me: *balance*. I was being told to play more, keep meditating, keep my energy up by eating properly and exercising, and to keep composing music—to participate in a variety of activities and interests. These hunches felt very accurate, and I have begun addressing my balance issues. When I am out of balance, my head is filled with too many thoughts that keep me out of the present moment and interfere with my intuition.

My Thoughts—

"Into thy hands, I commit
my spirit."

—Luke 23:43

Today, I missed out on a possible opportunity to engage someone as a future client. I was in a local bookstore when I saw a woman who looked very familiar. As she walked by me, I wanted to say something, but I was too cautious, though I was almost certain I had met her before. Later in the day I realized that she was a previous client, one that I had worked with many years ago. I know I need to act on my hunches, no matter how I am feeling. I didn't today, and I may have missed an opportunity. In what other situations in my life could I have listened to my intuition more, and acted on it?

My Thoughts—

"Attention is the ability we have to discriminate and to focus only on that which we want to perceive."

—Don Miguel Ruiz

David D. Dameron

Sometimes, even though we have set a goal or stated an intention, things don't work out the way we had envisioned. It's important in these times to trust the flow or the new direction and to ask in that moment, "Is this the path I'm meant to take?" It isn't always necessary to weigh the pros and cons of our decision. Instead, try asking the question and trusting the first answer that comes to you. I have always found the initial response to be accurate. When I allow my mind to start rationalizing, I cut off my intuition and cut myself off from the power it brings me.

My Thoughts—

"Yesterday ended last night."

—Raymond Charles Barber

I become better each day at paying attention to my thoughts and feelings. Several times every day, as part of my spiritual practice and routine, I ask Spirit what choice I should make. When I do, I feel an indescribable connection to my Higher Power. I'm filled with confidence about my life and the direction my life is taking. I also find listening to Spirit makes me a better teacher and advisor—it has helped me learn to listen intuitively instead of intellectually. I find my clients respond better to my advice. They are often surprised, as I am, at what I am able to intuit about them, their lives, their problems, and their dreams. How can I improve my intuitive listening even more?

My Thoughts—

"Trust God anyway."

—Bumper Sticker

Philosopher Immanuel Kant's writings use the word *phenomena* to describe things as they appear to us, rather than as they are in themselves. In other words, Kant was interested in understanding that what we observe through our senses may not always be the true reality of a thing or a situation. To get to the true nature of things in the outer world, it is useful to listen to our sixth sense—our intuitive capability. When we employ our intuitive faculty, then our physical eyes become our spiritual eyes. How can my intuitive ability show me the deeper meaning of my own physical reality?

My Thoughts—

"It is fallacy of the old schools to divide man into parcels, elements, thoughts, emotions, intuitions, etc. All human faculties consist of an interconnected whole."

—Alfred Korzybski

Sometimes my wife and I play a game that helps us connect with our intuition. When the telephone rings, we try to guess who is calling. Last night the telephone rang seven times, and we guessed correctly six times. There are times when we don't play well; but other times we are so tuned in that we are certain we've guessed correctly, even before we find out for sure. Think of your intuitional capability as a skill or a muscle that can be developed, like a golfer who practices to improve his or her swing, or someone who practices to learn to play a musical instrument. The more we practice with our intuitive faculty, the more honed it becomes.

My Thoughts—

"I cannot live my life
and explain it at the
same time."

—Anonymous

David D. Dameron

Often the people I train have trouble understanding the difference between their intuition and their intellect. If you have to think about something, you are using your intellect. Intuition is a bit more difficult to define. I looked up the word *intuition* in *Roget's Thesaurus* and here are some of the entries: *sense, sixth sense, hunch, feeling, instinct, insight, "feeling in one's bones," "gut instinct," vibes, inkling, perception, discernment, apprehension.* Throughout the day, jot down the thoughts you've had and the decisions you've made. At the end of the day, look over your list. Were you working from your intellect or your intuition? In what situations is it appropriate for me to use intellect, and in what areas could my life benefit from my using intuition?

My Thoughts—

"The kingdom of God is within; the place whereon we stand is holy ground."

—Joel Goldsmith

I woke up today and knew intuitively that it was time to let go of some of my clients. I had been feeling that events in my life were urging me to make a change. I wasted some of the morning rationalizing my decision and worrying about the past. I found myself wishing I were more centered emotionally about this change, and I kept worrying I was forcing the change because of bad choices I'd made in the past. Then I realized I was listening to my intellect rather than my intuition and living in the past instead of living in the moment. My intuition is about the present—the only real moment that exists. My intuition is about being directed by my higher self—my divine self, which never has failed me. I must admit that at times it takes courage to listen to my intuition, but when I do, I never regret it.

My Thoughts—

"Do what you feel in
your heart to be right."

—Anonymous

David D. Dameron

One of my clients, a human resources manager for a manufacturing company, came up to me today and thanked me for helping one of her employees. At first I didn't know what she meant; then she reminded me that I had introduced her employee to a woman at my wife's school. They began dating and then fell in love. The manager said her employee was happier and performing better at work. I thought back to the time when I introduced them, and I remembered I had a strong feeling these two people should come together. I seldom feel any inclination to be a "matchmaker," and I realized my impulse was evidence of the Divine's hand in this situation. My intuition knew these two people were meant to fall in love. I'm glad I listened to my inner voice—and so are they!

My Thoughts—

"In every moment of genuine love we are dwelling in God and God in us."

—Paul Tillich

My intuition possibly saved the life of one of my dogs today. My dogs often suffer from minor stomach problems or a sore paw, and they generally recover quickly. But today was different. I felt something was not right with my dog Rosie. She didn't look different in any way, but my intuition was telling me something was very wrong. I rushed her off to the vet, and found she had a severe case of food poisoning. The vet told me it was good thing I had brought her in as quickly as I did. I was very glad I'd been practicing hearing the voice of my intuition and acting on it. In what other situations have I been glad I acted on my intuition? In what cases did I fail to trust a hunch and come to wish I had?

My Thoughts—

"Our true home is the present moment. The true miracle is not to walk on water ... the true miracle is to walk on the earth in the present moment."

—Thich Nhat Hanh

David D. Dameron

My wife and I left on a trip to Michigan today, and I was having some conflicted feelings about our house/dog sitter, though I couldn't identify the reason for my unease. Instead of stopping to tune into these feelings and discuss them with my wife, we rushed off to the airport to catch our plane. When we arrived in Michigan, I tried to call the sitter at our house, expecting to find her there caring for the dogs—but there was no answer. I tried again and again, and finally reached her at the end of the day. She had mistakenly thought we did not need her to be at our house until evening, and that meant the dogs had been locked up all day. I was really upset with myself that I had not listened and acted on my intuition.

My Thoughts—

"One should lie empty, open, choiceless as a beach—waiting for a gift from the sea."

—Anne Morrow

When I am feeling in conflict about a situation or decision I need to make, I know that I am in my intellect. Only in my intellect do I feel blocked, indecisive, and out of touch with the present moment. So I have worked to develop my intuition, learning how to receive and how to listen. It isn't easy; Western men and women are so programmed to rationalize and analyze. But when I do analyze and rationalize, I feel cutoff from my spirit. That doesn't feel good or right, and it teaches me to trust my intuition and work to better learn when it is appropriate to use my analytical nature and when to rely upon my intuition. In what situations should I use my intellect and in what situations would it be beneficial to use my intuition?

My Thoughts—

"Every morning, consider doing
this: Light a candle. Sit down.
Close your eyes. Be with God."

—Marianne Williamson

David D. Dameron

My spiritual teachers told me that we are never given a challenge that is beyond our ability to overcome, though the challenge may seem too difficult. I realize that one of God's gifts to us in such a situation is our intuitive capabilities. If things look really bleak and you do not know what to do, try utilizing your intuition. Learn to recognize it and its voice. Learn to honor and to love it. Learn how to bring your focus and awareness into the present moment and ask what you should do. Then, act on your first impulse. Your heart will validate the decision you make.

My Thoughts—

"You are never given a wish without also being given the power to make it true. You may have to work for it, however."

—Richard Bach

CHAPTER FOUR:

POWER

"Well, you won't discover it by waiting for divine revelation, absolute certainty, a mystical vision, or the voice of God. So don't weigh ideas or wonder; don't doubt your direction or depend on others to tell you what you should or shouldn't do. Go toward what attracts or excites or inspires you—toward what touches your heart."

—Dan Millman, *The Laws of Spirit*

When I consciously began my spiritual exploration in the late seventies, I became aware of some of the challenges it presented in examining and changing my life, my assumptions, and my approaches. Career, money, relationships, and my health were all areas that I knew I needed to explore and heal.

Little did I know what my most challenging spiritual experience was going to be in this lifetime—a challenge wholly unanticipated and unlike anything I could have ever imagined.

My real spiritual challenge turned out to be REMODELING—that's right, the remodeling of my house. That doesn't exactly sound like a spiritual topic, does it? But if you can stop laughing for a moment, please know that I am truly serious. If you have ever gone through a major remodeling project, you probably know exactly what I am talking about.

Toward the end of 2002, my wife and I decided that we would remodel our home to give us more space to pursue our creative interests. Being a teacher of time and project management workshops, I was certain that planning and executing a remodeling project would be easy for me.

I remember that, during the time we were planning the project, I had lunch with one of my clients, who was bemoaning the problems he was having with a new pool installation in his backyard. I boastfully told my client that, if I ever engaged in a house or yard project, my management skills would save me from ever having the problems he was having.

My wife and I interviewed several contractors and finally chose one who had come highly recommended. We went over our expectations with him, making clear the details of what we wanted done. I later came to realize it was unfortunate that many of those details were only discussed verbally, instead of being captured in written form as well.

The contractor was slower in getting us a final contract than we would have liked, but he finally submitted it, and my wife and I reviewed it. Reading it, I kept having a nagging thought that the contract was not detailed enough. Then another voice inside my head said, "Don't be anal-retentive about this," and because I was anxious to start on the work, I listened to that second voice. At that point, the contract was on its third revision, and I could tell that the contractor did not want to draft any more paperwork on this project.

So we accepted the contract. He told us that we did not have to move out, as his subcontractors could work around us. I told him I was self-employed and worked from home, so knowing their schedule, and keeping that schedule, was important to me.

Well, the first day was hectic. Workers everywhere. Music boxes on high volume. Several questions for me each hour. By the end of the day, when my wife came home from work, my hair was standing on end (from wanting to pull it out!), my eyes were popping out of my head, and the dogs looked the same way. And this was just Day One.

As the work continued, we realized that the subcontractor had installed the wrong windows. When we confronted the contractor about this, he pointed out what the contract said. We had talked verbally about the style of the window we wanted, but the contract did not reflect that conversation. So we were stuck with the windows.

Over the next two months of this project, there were several "I said, you said" conversations, and each one was a painful reminder of the voice—my intuition—that had warned me to get it all in writing and my decision not to listen to that voice.

Because I had not listened to my intuition, I was now stuck with the work being done. I was angry with the contractor, and he knew it. But the person I was most angry with was myself.

The work the remodeling company did was outstanding but way behind schedule, and I began to wonder if our lives would ever return to normal. The whole experience culminated on a day two months after the remodel began, when I gave the remodelers an ultimatum to be out of our house within a week. They told me my deadline was impossible to meet, and I contemplated being left with an unusable, partially remodeled house. But I was adamant—and the workers finished the work within the week I'd given them.

What I was accomplishing with the ultimatum was taking my power back. Instead of continuing to attempt to define the details, instead of continuing to waste my breath on the delays in scheduling, instead of trying over and over to control the noise in the house and to control a number of other uncontrollable elements, I finally chose to be direct and firm. I had reached my limit, made up my mind to speak up, and "put my foot down." I was clear and to the point about something I *could* control—whether these workers entered my house again after one week had passed—and I finally accomplished exactly what I wanted to accomplish.

- - - - - - - - - - - - - -

The remodeling project served as a mirror for me, and is the subject of this chapter, which is about *power*. Normally, one would think of power as something you possess to dominate another. But the power I am referring to goes much deeper.

The remodeling project did not go well for me for several reasons that went beyond the contractor himself. One reason goes back to the conversation I had with my client at lunch, which I related at the beginning of this chapter. This remodeling project taught me the price of arrogance. When I thought I could plan and execute a project without hitches because I teach efficient processes in my consulting and training, I was setting myself up. I was actually giving away my power by suggesting I could control every aspect of this project, because that goal was in no way in my control.

On another level, I was out of integrity with myself, and hence diminished my power when I did not require the contract to be more specific. I also should have spoken up about the noise factor and interruptions to voice my preferences, but I did not. I did not want to offend the contractor and subcontractors, and in acting out of a desire not to offend, I robbed myself of my power.

The contractor served me well—not as a contractor, but as a teacher. His actions worked as a mirror to reflect things inside of myself that I needed to look at. In other words, he played his part well and showed me things about myself that I needed to address.

On a deeper level, this project was as much about "remodeling" myself as it was about remodeling my house. I had been working on some major internal changes during this time in an attempt to shed myself of habits and patterns that were not serving my spiritual growth. One of the patterns I had wanted to change was to begin to be more authentic with my clients—to learn to speak up without worrying so much about offending. Another area I had been trying to change was to remind myself that some things were beyond my control. I wanted to remember that I could not control people's reactions or how some things happened in my life. So remodeling the house became a metaphor for the spiritual remodeling I was doing inside myself, and it was quite appropriate that spiritual lessons came to me through the contractor I hired to rebuild.

As I explore the subject of power in this chapter, please remember your own power. You are a divine being. You have established values and beliefs, and you are entitled to hold them and to express them. You must have the courage to speak your heart and act in a way that matches your values and your beliefs—that is the essence, the nature, of true power, the power of your divine existence.

In claiming your own power, it is also important to set boundaries in terms of your expectations from people. For example, if you do not want someone smoking in your house, then if they start to do so, you need to speak up and honor the boundary you have established as important to you.

As we evolve in our consciousness or our awareness, we realize that the first person we must be true to in our lives is our own self. That is integrity. Acting on and listening to your divine guidance is true power. When I pointed this viewpoint out to a good friend one day, he told me that his first priority was not to himself but to God. My response to him was, "What is the difference?"

True power does not seek to dominate or control another. True power does not try to bring harm to another. As you will discover, true power is about being PRESENT with your spirit and letting every action and decision flow from this sacred place inside yourself. You can then see the sacred in life.

- - - - - - - - - - - - - -

I wrote in my journal today that I needed to remind myself to stay in the moment. When I reflect on things that have happened in the past that I have regretted, I lose some of my power. I become sad or depressed about something I cannot change, something that has already happened. When I worry about something that might happen in the future, I again diminish my power by giving attention to something which has not even happened and may never happen. I am reminded of the saying, "We'll cross that bridge when we have to," as a good reminder that the best time to deal with a situation is in the moment, when it arises. My point here is that I feel most in connection with my spirit and I am more centered when I am totally present and focused on the moment.

My Thoughts—

"There is never a time and place when we are powerless—there are merely times we forget who we truly are."

—Doreen Virtue

David D. Dameron

I made a very poor presentation to a prospective client today. I felt "off" going into the meeting, and I realized I was worried about my mother-in-law's health and about how my wife was handling the challenges of the situation. I felt my posture and my composure were affected because I allowed my mind and emotions to stray from my focus, from what I needed to do in order to make an effective presentation. This experience reminded me to be present and focused, so as not to lose my power worrying about things over which I have no control.

My Thoughts—

"Keep fresh before me the moments of my high resolve, that in fair weather or in foul, in good times or in tempests . . . I may not forget that to which my life is committed."

—Howard Thurman

I met with one of my clients today, a senior executive of a corporation. We spent some time talking about true abundance, and we also talked about how he had lost some of his passion for his career. Watching his reaction to our conversation, I realized we were exploring some areas sensitive to him. I also realized how wonderful it felt to be able to speak my truth with the hope that my insights would help him. While I could recognize his reaction to our conversation, I was not worried about how he was receiving what we were talking about. What I found most interesting was how differently we each looked at abundance. He thought abundance was about money. My viewpoint was that abundance encompassed an attitude about life. I suggested he read my first book, *Remembering Our Spirit*, for ways to contemplate a broader understanding of *abundance*. For myself, I came away from our conversation with a good example of how to be supportive of my client at the same time that I spoke authentically and without becoming over concerned with his emotions around our discussion—an area over which I had no control.

My Thoughts—

"The individual is a stream whose source is hidden."

—Ralph Waldo Emerson

David D. Dameron

I learned a wonderful technique to help me stay in my power. Before leaving the house to start my day, I imagine myself being inside a sphere of light much like an energy field. I imagine the sphere protecting me from taking on some of the negative energies that I encounter on a day-to-day basis with people with whom I work. You may be aware of feeling drained after you've been with people who are negative; or maybe you find yourself participating in negativity yourself, with others or during a particularly negative business meeting. When you feel drained, you may have taken on the negative energy that was being generated. The antidote is to surround yourself with positive energy. Try imagining this protective sphere and thinking of it as an expression of confidence and focus and being fully present, inspired, and enthusiastic with every person or situation you encounter.

My Thoughts—

"Knowledge is power."

—Francis Bacon

I stand firm in the truth that, regardless of appearances, I will seek to find the Divine in all of my affairs and in all the people I encounter. When I encounter something negative, whether it is my own thought or something external, I put my hand over my heart and affirm with feeling that I am an aspect of God and that my purpose is to seek a positive connection with everyone I meet. I release any negative thoughts I am having, and I affirm that I am protected and loved and that everything I desire has already been provided.

My Thoughts—

"All the world loves a lover."

—Proverb

David D. Dameron

I am really struggling today. Because of the remodeling, problems with my parent's estate, and feeling some financial pressure because my business is in a slow period, I told some friends today that I could not play golf with them. Instead of being truthful, though, I made up a story to avoid exposing how I was really feeling. I felt I would let them down if I told them the truth. I realized that I was giving away my power in this instance by not being truthful. Sometimes the ways we give away our power are so subtle. I did not like myself today, and determined I would not let telling falsehoods rob me of my power again.

My Thoughts—

"This above all: To thine own self be true, and it must follow as the night and the day, thou canst not be false to any man."

—William Shakespeare

One of the techniques I use to enhance my power is to develop a mission statement for myself. This statement establishes my purpose in life. It also includes those values which are important to me. Often I review my mission statement by looking at my journal and reflecting upon what has happened to me during the day or how I have reacted to a situation. When I have remained true to my mission statement, I congratulate myself. If I have strayed from my beliefs, I look for ways to improve in the future. Do you have a mission statement for your life? Do you have a set of values by which you live your life?

My Thoughts—

"The authentic self is the
soul made visible."

—Sarah Ban Breathnach

In the relationships I had before I got married, I sometimes diminished my power. I found that I would violate boundaries I had established for what I wanted in a relationship. For example, if I decided that I did not want to date someone with young children, I found that I would overlook that boundary if I met someone I was attracted to. But though I thought my attraction to someone overcame my reserves, as we became more involved I began to realize that my original approach was the right one—I did not want the responsibility of raising more children (since I had two of my own). I have learned to become faithful to my boundaries. When I am, I live my life in integrity, and integrity is power!

My Thoughts—

"Meditate on your Self. Honor and worship your own inner being. God dwells within you as you."

—Swami Muktananda

I have found that, in certain situations, fear is behind my not being true to my power. For example, there have been times when I was afraid to approach my kids about something, fearing their reaction. As teenagers, they sometimes did not want to be engaged on certain topics. In addition to fearing reactions, I realized sometimes I allow people's inappropriate behavior to continue because I am afraid of creating conflict with them. When I allow my fears to control a situation, I do not feel powerful. I need to become very present in these situations and speak my truth with love and caring. I cannot control how someone might react to me, but I can control how I deliver a message. What other examples can I think of in which I sometimes let my fears dominate?

My Thoughts—

"It's rigged—everything, in your favor. So there's nothing to worry about."

—Jalaludin Rumi

David D. Dameron

Today I hired a young man to do some yard work for me. I had felt sorry for him since it was obvious he had a learning disability. He also said that he was trying to start his own business doing yard work. As he proceeded to work on my yard, it was very apparent that he did not have the capability to do so, nor did he have the tools to do the job. I realized that I should have asked more questions before he started and before I committed to hiring him, but at that point I did not want to hurt his feelings by getting upset with him. I finally had to send him home because of the poor work he was doing. In the end, I felt powerless. Instead of taking control of this situation early on, it had gotten out of control because I had been afraid of offending the young man. In what other ways have I given away my power?

My Thoughts—

"Divide and rule."

—Proverb

I felt good about myself today. One of the boundaries I've set with clients is that I have a certain "lead time" I keep in regards to accepting new projects. A prospective client, who knew my requested lead time, wanted to do some business with me that did not keep that boundary. I knew I could use the money, but I had little enthusiasm for the project and I also wanted to honor the boundary I had set, so I said no. Although my prospective client was disappointed, I really felt in my power today. I felt very focused and present. In what other situations have I learned to set my boundaries and say no?

My Thoughts—

"I've got to admit it's getting better. It's getting better all the time."

—John Lennon and Paul McCartney

David D. Dameron

My value system was tested today. I encountered a situation with a group of my more enjoyable clients. I had discovered that there was some illegal activity being conducted on their premises. When I made the executives aware of the activity, they were upset, but they were not willing to hold some of the individuals involved with the illegal activity accountable. I recognized that the executives were giving their power away in this situation. They felt that by firing the individuals they would hurt their customer service and impact getting their orders out on time, so they chose to counsel the individuals involved. I have boundaries of my own around ethics, and, in response, I gave this company my notice that I would no longer be working with them. As much as I enjoyed working with this company and the fact that they paid me well, I had to be true to my values and my ethics. I was in my power today.

My Thoughts—

"You don't have power
if you surrender all your
principles—you   have
office."

—Ron Todd, union leader

Visualization is a very powerful technique athletes sometimes use to help them perform at a higher level. The athletes envision in their minds that they are performing in a certain event, and they visualize a positive outcome. For example, a golfer might visualize a perfect swing and a low golf score. A basketball player might visualize successfully passing and shooting in a game, leading to a winning score. You and I can also make use of effective visualization in our professional and personal affairs. Visualization sets our intentions in motion. When we are acting on our intentions, we are present, in the moment, and focused. Try this technique on a regular basis. What were the results of your efforts?

My Thoughts—

"Imagination is more important than knowledge."

—Albert Einstein

David D. Dameron

I am teaching a new workshop on stress today. This workshop really challenges individuals to look at their lives in a different way. I am teaching this first class to a group of people who do not explore or share new ideas very easily. At first, I had some fears about how they would receive this class. But I decided to visualize them receiving the class in a positive way, as well as visualizing myself imparting the instruction with confidence and enthusiasm. I did not allow myself to worry about how they would receive my instruction. As it turned out, they loved the workshop and found the material very helpful in their lives. I taught today from a place of personal power and conviction, and it felt wonderful.

My Thoughts—

"And he who sees me has already seen the one who sent me."

—John 12:45

We all wear masks that conceal our insecurities. Here are some examples of the masks we may wear:

•An individual who would really like to change careers because he or she is unhappy instead puts on the front that they are happy with what they are doing

•A person who blames someone else for their problems and refuses to accept their own responsibility (This is called the victim mask.)

•Someone who is insecure, but hides that by being overly boastful

•Individuals who express their true feelings about a person through the use of inappropriate humor, instead of being honest and stating how they feel

All of these are examples of people who are giving up their power instead of making empowered choices or taking appropriate actions in their lives. What masks do you wear, and how do these masks diminish your personal power?

My Thoughts—

"Let this mind be in you, which was also in Jesus Christ."

—Philippians 2:5

Power and self-esteem are intimately connected. When you make choices out of fear, you lose power and connection with your spirit, and that can affect how you feel about yourself and how you perceive your outer world. Affirm each day, "I am honest and obedient to my truth. I choose to live my life in love and integrity. I am an aspect of God, and I best serve people in my life by being true to my spirit."

My Thoughts—

"Nothing real can be threatened. Nothing unreal exists."

—*A Course in Miracles*

CHAPTER FIVE:

FREEDOM

"You are led through your lifetime by the inner learning creature, the playful spiritual being that is your real self. Don't turn away from possible futures before you're certain. You don't have anything to learn from them. You're always free to change your mind and choose a different future, or a different past."

—Richard Bach, *Illusions*

Recently I had lunch with one of my clients, and she told me about her adventures as a Peace Corps worker. She had traveled to several third-world countries and told me of what she had witnessed: extreme poverty, starving children, and parents struggling to make ends meet. She told me about houses with no running water or electricity. She painted a very bleak picture, one which pulled at my heartstrings. As a result of her experience, when my friend returned to America she saw our society with different eyes. She was appalled to see the emphasis on materialism in the society in which she had grown up.

Her feeling was that Americans should be more aware of third-world conditions. She also felt our extraordinarily high quality of living had caused us to lose sight of what is truly important in life.

She ended her tirade on American life by saying that we should be ashamed of our focus on the material aspects of life and that we should find ways to help these third-world countries rise from their poverty.

As I listened intently to what she was saying, I felt a number of responses that I wanted to express to her; but I have chosen instead to write about what I was feeling.

Although I appreciated her point of view, my opinions about America and our material wealth were quite a bit different from hers. As I gathered my thoughts to write them down, I thought about freedom and what it means to be American. I fully realize that we are envied and despised by much of the world for our standard of living and our political and military policies. But if one looks beneath the surface, what America stands for is based on more than how we live or what our government does.

America is an idea—more precisely, America is about possibilities. Through creativity and hard work, this country has created the most affluent nation on the face of the planet. I often write about *divine inheritance.* In one sense, America is claiming its divine inheritance: our ability to manifest a high quality of living.

No one on this planet should be living in poverty or prevented from having the opportunities which are afforded to us in the United States. But political policies and lack of social reform on the part of certain governments leave the majority of the world's population struggling day to day just to make a living.

I believe that repressive governments are not only physically starving their populations, but they are spiritually starving them. When your day-to-day existence consists of trying to find food to eat or shelter for your family, you have no inclination, and no energy to spare, to think about God.

David D. Dameron

America, too, has problems. Daily we face poverty, educational challenges, and a number of other social issues. We must deal with racism, corporate greed, misuse of power, and environmental challenges. At times, our political and military policies are not in the best interest of our own population or that of the world. We are overtaxed, and our debt and deficit are mounting.

But—what we do have in this country is *freedom*. We are free to vote and to use that vote, if we so choose, to put individuals into office who will initiate policies that are in the best interest of our entire society. We have the freedom to choose jobs we want to work in, or to create our own businesses. We have the freedom to worship as we choose. We have the freedom to protest our differences and our viewpoints. So in its truest sense, freedom is the power to make *choices*. The quality of those choices then determines the quality of our lives.

But America is not exempt from losing its freedom; with freedom comes the responsibility to steward it well.

I am not unaware of the terrible conditions some people on this planet endure, and I have deep compassion for them. We as individuals and as a country must search for peaceful ways to encourage other governments to give individuals greater freedom and greater power of choice. We must help our own government and other nations to create opportunities for citizens of the world to have a higher quality of life through creation of healthy communities.

All of us on this planet are interconnected, and the great thing about America is that we are showing people what is possible in terms of living lives that offer freedom and choice. But that demonstration is not enough. We must be thankful for the quality of our own lives, and work to bring that quality of life to others. By the lives we live and the choices we make, we can show the world the myriad of possibilities that exist for freedom and happiness. Freedom has its challenges, but it is also our door of opportunity; we can choose to walk through that door and fulfill our potential by living our life from our divinity.

- - - - - - - - - - - - - - -

This chapter is about *freedom* and what it means to be able to manifest our divine potential. Can we use the power of the choices we make to benefit others as well as ourselves? Can we look at what benefits the whole instead of only considering our own needs?

Although America is about possibilities, we can lose our freedom if we do not steward it well. We must use the power of our vote in this country. We must hold our public officials accountable. We must speak up about issues that are important to us.

Freedom is our divine birthright, and to steward that freedom, we are being asked at a core level to live our lives in harmony and peace. We are being asked to assist all people of the world to rise from feeling weak and disenfranchised to being empowered and inspired to live a higher quality of life. To achieve the true power of freedom is to attain self-mastery and self-realization.

Change begins one person at a time, with one person who is willing to stand up for their freedom, speak their truth, and act in the best interest of the whole. Freedom honors diversity. Freedom is the true expression of our divinity. Freedom is available to each of us in this very moment, if we can develop the self-awareness to be able to understand its nature and its possibilities.

So, rather than argue with my friend, I chose not to diminish her for her beliefs, to which she, like every divine human being, is entitled. Instead, I thanked her silently for giving me the opportunity to think about freedom. But I make no excuses for my country because of our affluence. We have problems, but I make no apologies for our ability to manifest a high quality of life. We are demonstrating to the rest of the world the infinite possibilities freedom offers.

Freedom is an idea and a possibility. To sustain it, we must also accept the huge responsibility to manage our freedom properly, or risk losing it.

I leave you with this quote from the Declaration of Independence; to me, it embodies the spirit of freedom. I have capitalized those words that I suggest you really should reflect upon.

> "We hold these TRUTHS
> to be self-evident, that all
> men are created EQUAL,
> that they are endowed BY
> THEIR CREATOR with
> certain unalienable Rights,
> that among these are Life,
> LIBERTY, and the Pursuit of
> Happiness."

- - - - - - - - - - - - - -

David D. Dameron

Recently I came across some articles in a magazine that were written by individuals who were incarcerated. The major point or each of their essays was that they lived in more than physical prisons. They also were locked into their own internal prisons. These individuals truly became aware of the choices they had made in their lives only when their freedom had been taken away and they were really forced to look at themselves and the results of their choices. The authors of these articles had made the connection that their external worlds were a mirror of their internal worlds. What choices have you made that have kept your real spirit locked inside your jail—the jail of your spirit? Have you lied, cheated, stolen, been afraid to speak up, been fearful? When have you been afraid to face the truth of a situation? Do you believe it would be useful to contemplate the way we create our own internal prisons by allowing bad choices to dominate our lives?

My Thoughts—

"No one knows how far it is from nothingness to God. As long as you cling to your self you will wander left and right . . . but if, once freed from your self, you will finally get down to work, this door will open to you within two minutes."

—Hakim Abu'L-Majd

The articles I wrote of yesterday, written by prisoners who had discovered the connection between being in prison physically and being in prison emotionally and spiritually, have so many lessons to offer. I am reminded of some of my clients whose fears drive the choices they make. One is afraid to confront his boss over the way his boss humiliates some of his managers in front of others; another client feels she cannot find a job in which she can feel passionate about her work. If we do not recognize and control our own fears, we all create the non-existent phantoms that haunt our lives and the prisons that cage us. In each moment, I have a choice and I can ask myself, "Is my choice at this present time based on fear? Does it free my spirit or does it confine my spirit?"

My Thoughts—

"He whose joy is within, whose pleasure is within, and whose light is within, that devotee, being well and established in the Supreme, attains to absolute freedom."

—*The Bhagavad-Gita*

David D. Dameron

Freedom and power are interestingly intertwined. I find that when a clergyman, politician, corporate leader, or civil servant professes to be serving the best interests of others, I am skeptical. All too often we have seen these people misuse their power by deceiving or controlling others. They may call what they wield *power,* but it is not real power. I believe that true power lies inside of us and does not reside in any one person *outside* of us. When we can come to that realization, we are truly free. We are no longer looking outside of our own selves, our own intuition and heart, to direct our lives. In this new awareness we can better discern who is or is not working in our best interests. To whom have I looked outside of myself for direction in my life, and what impetus led me to allow this person to control what I think?

My Thoughts—

"Fear always springs
from ignorance."

—Ralph Waldo Emerson

A great technique that I learned today is to *name* your fears. Some common fears that I encounter when working with others or myself are:

- fear of offending
- fear of conflict
- fear of expressing how you feel
- fear of being alone
- fear of public speaking
- fear of searching for the truth
- fear of dying

When you discover one of your fears, imagine what your life would be like if you embodied the opposite of that fear. Ask yourself what could be the worst thing that could happen if you faced your fear and what you would do if that worst-case scenario came about. The more you face your fears the more you free your spirit. What fears do you finally need to face, and how will you do so?

My Thoughts—

"So free we seem, so fettered fast we are!"

—Robert Browning

I have written many times about two words that were written in ancient times, words that were and remain a guide to living a life of high quality and enlightenment: *know thyself.* So often, our lives offer us experiences that hold valuable insights, if only we can recognize that insight and apply it. If we apply that insight in a constructive way, it becomes wisdom, and wisdom then becomes freedom. In what situations in my life have I had experiences that seemed to offer me something that I could not quite grasp?

My Thoughts—

"Why does He wish to be prayed to endlessly for that which He has already decreed to grant or not to grant, since being immutable He cannot change His decrees?"

—Desiderius Erasmus

Many spiritual texts, including my own writings, often state that *everything that we could possibly desire has already been provided.* Whether we ask for forgiveness in a situation when speaking to our divinity or desire something in our lives, if we can envision what we desire and feel that we deserve it, then, hopefully, we can realize that what we desire has already been given to us. We only need believe that it has. Belief opens a door inside ourselves that lets us access healing. When you fully realize the power of your own belief, and know that power is real, you are free. Then you will see the sacred in life!

My Thoughts—

"He is thus the grand seigneur, the spiritual aristocrat who is so sure of the position given to him by birth that he has no need to condescend or put on airs."

—Alan Watts

David D. Dameron

I once heard a speaker talk about the idea of *first cause*—the intelligence and power that created everything we know in the universe. He said the first cause was omnipresent, omnipotent, and omniscient. He then tried to help us understand that there is nothing that has happened to us in the past that cannot be transmuted into a positive energy. He also pointed out that the universe is designed such that nothing we could possibly attract in the future could be beyond what we are equipped to handle. Every challenge has a solution that is within our grasp. Since we, too, are an aspect of this first cause, this all-powerful intelligence is present to all of us and available to us if we ask it for insight and are willing to listen to its answers. Our choice making then becomes a reflection of how well we establish an awareness of this first cause, or our own divinity.

My Thoughts—

"I have only one purpose: to make man free; to urge him toward freedom; to help him to break away from all limitations, for that alone will give him external happiness, will give him unconditional realization of Self."

—J. Krishnamurti

112

I celebrated Independence Day in March today. I had one of those "aha" moments that made my spirit feel free. I came to a full realization that what I send out returns to me, and made the connection between that concept and the quantum physics theory that our universe is curved in nature; because it is curved, our thoughts and actions return to us. I realized I cannot fool the power within. Our lives, our destinies, are designed to evolve toward first cause. As part of that design, when we find fault, criticize, or do harm to someone, the shape of the universe naturally returns those same things to us. The "aha" that made my spirit feel free was the realization that, by the same token, when I choose to live my life in love, peace, and compassion, those things are naturally returned to me as well.

My Thoughts—

"So think as if your every thought were to be etched in fire upon the sky for all and everything to see. For so, in truth, it is."

—Mikhail Naimy, *The Book of Mirdad*

I had to advise one of my clients today against interfering in other people's lives. She was trying to get involved between a father and his daughter, and she was compounding their problems by not allowing the two of them to work things out. I told her that sometimes people have the right to experience life as they need to, even if our perception is that they are making a mistake. In following their own belief in how to behave and respond, they hopefully learn valuable life lessons they needed to learn. I suggested that, in this case, instead of interfering, she envision both of them fulfilled and coming to a positive conclusion with their challenge. To do otherwise is to interfere. We do not have to solve everyone's challenges. We have enough to do just dealing with our own daily challenges.

My Thoughts—

"Freedom is the right to
tell people what they do
not want to hear."

—George Orwell

Each day, affirm with great feeling, "I live life with great certainty and confidence; I stand firm in my beliefs and act with great integrity in all things I do during the day. I handle any challenges I encounter this day with patience, and seek to find the positive in whatever is happening. I am present and in the moment with my spirit, and I know that I best serve my spirit by being centered in love and truth. I am a divine being, and I love life. I am truly free."

My Thoughts—

"So speak as if the world entire were but a single ear intent on hearing what you say. And so, in truth, it is."

—Mikhail Naimy, *The Book of Mirdad*

David D. Dameron

    I was asked today who inspires me and who best represents how I feel about freedom. I responded with a long list of people. Besides people close to me personally, the more famous people who inspire are individuals like Oprah Winfrey, Steven Spielberg, Jimmy Carter, Brian Wilson, Richard Gere, Bono, John Travolta, and the Dixie Chicks. Please understand that it is not that I agree all of the time with what some of these people say or how they lead their lives; but I do respect how they choose to express themselves, and the freedom that allows them to do so, whether I agree with them or not. These people express themselves through their spirits, and their example can help all of us to realize that we, too, can stand up for what we believe. Who, by expressing their spirit, inspires you?

My Thoughts—

"God has many names though He is one being."

—Aristotle

Today I have been reflecting on how often I allow my thoughts to wander, and especially how unproductive it is to wander into negativity. I become unfocused and unmotivated when I allow myself to indulge in negative self-talk. In those moments I become a prisoner to my thoughts. And yet, how I yearn to experience Spirit in each moment! This is freedom to me. When I am in connection with my spirit and present in this very moment, I feel free. I feel powerful. In what ways can I remind myself to stay present in the moment, and approach each moment positively?

My Thoughts—

"The condition upon which God hath given liberty to man is eternal vigilance."

—John Philpot Curran

David D. Dameron

There are things beyond the material world, things we cannot see. Inside ourselves is a place that can never be touched by adversity or fear. The Divine has given us a sacred place called *hope*. As the old saying goes, "Hope springs eternal." We must have faith in that divine gift of hope, and by it know that we are never alone in our struggles. Embracing the feeling of hope connects us to understanding freedom. Science says that energy can never be destroyed. As with energy and Spirit, hope is eternal!

My Thoughts—

"True freedom is won and lost in the heart."

—Mikhail Naimy, *The Book of Mirdad*

There is only one true choice in life, and that is to follow the will of our divinity. No matter how many choices it may seem we have, free choice only allows us to practice our choice making in one of two ways: by choosing to follow the will of our ego, or by choosing to follow the will of our spirit. Our destiny and our purpose have already been "etched in stone." It may take us thousands of years to realize the truth of this, but once we can embrace our divinity, then we realize the purpose of life: to become one with the Divine. The day will come when humanity will be released from the shackles of ignorance. On that day, we will embrace diversity and dignity and realize we are truly one. On that day, we will celebrate our independence and there will be peace on earth.

My Thoughts—

"And the chief captain answered, with a great sum obtained I this freedom. And Paul said, But I was free born."

—Acts 22:28

CHAPTER SIX:

JOY

"Joy is the very highest state. It is the exaltation of soul as physical pleasure is the exaltation of the body. But it is the true emotional state of man, born from his inner release into the truth of his being."

—Baird T. Spalding,
Life and Teachings of the Masters of the Far East

Any of you who have had children, or who know of those who have had them, may have heard of the expression, "Watch out for the terrible twos." In the case of my own childhood, the saying could have been modified to, "Watch out for the terrible threes." During these years of growth, children can be very challenging, and my own parents, from what I have been told, were not excused from those hurdles with me. But though my parents seem to have attempted to bridle my enthusiasm and curiosity, I know being three was nevertheless a time of magic in my life.

At that time we were living in the suburbs of Louisville, Kentucky, on Hemingway Road. My father was self-employed and had his own janitorial supply business, and my mom worked as a bookkeeper for the family business. My two older brothers were in school, and I had a maid/sitter, Dorothy, whose rare opportunity and challenge was to watch me while she did chores around the house.

I mention the words "rare opportunity and challenge" because two other sitters had quit out of frustration they experienced over trying to control my behavior. One day I was riding my red tractor in front of our house, and periodically, Dorothy would step outside the front door to make sure I was still in sight. She knew my reputation for disappearing in a moment's notice.

I remember this day as if it were yesterday. It was a wonderful spring day with clear, blue skies. As I was riding my tractor up and down the street, still under Dorothy's scrutiny, a feeling came over me that I very much wanted to go see my grandmother. Without giving any thought to Dorothy or possible consequences to my rear end, I turned my red tractor around and took off for my grandmother's house.

A three-year-old on a red tractor—needless to say, this sudden and daring feat of impulse was not going to be an easy task. My grandmother's house was almost two miles away, and I had to traverse several streets and a major thoroughfare to get to her house on Brown's Lane. I remember the traffic as I peddled down the sidewalks and crossed the street, intent on reaching her house. My thoughts were in no way about Dorothy or my impending imprisonment; I was wholly in the moment and thinking about how excited grandmother would be to see me.

I loved going to my grandmother's house, and have wonderful memories of playing in the many rooms there, and of her famous cookie jar in the kitchen, my fingerprints on it evidence of how often I accessed its contents. After peddling for some time, my little legs started to get tired, but I did finally arrive at my destination. I parked my tractor on the front lawn, ran up to the house, and knocked on the door.

My grandmother came to the door, and her expression was priceless when she saw me. She opened the door to let me in while hugging me until I could not breathe, and she asked me where my mother was. I answered that I thought she was at work. My grandmother's next question was how did I get here? I turned around and proudly pointed to my red tractor parked in the front yard.

At that point, much to my surprise, my grandmother ran down the hallway with her arms flailing in the air, saying "Oh my God, oh my God!" I had heard this three-letter word *God* before, and I made the connection to the church we attended across the street from her house, where this person named God lived. I was kind of interested in meeting him. But I had heard this person God mentioned before by my dad when he got upset with me, and I remember thinking God's last name must be *Dammit*.

Well, what happened next was a blur. My grandmother called my mother at work, and she came to get me to take me home. I could not understand why I had not been offered any cookies this time, especially considering how much I had done to get to my grandmother's house. When my mother arrived, she had Dorothy in the car. Everyone was hysterical. They were yelling at me and telling me I could have been killed. I do remember not being able to sit down for days for some reason. And to think, all I did was go and visit my own grandmother!

- - - - - - - - - - - - - - -

This chapter is about the subject of *joy*. The synonyms the thesaurus gives for joy are *happiness, delight, euphoria, bliss, glee, jubilance, rapture,* and *transport*. All of these synonyms describe how I felt at the age of three.

The significance of my red tractor story became more evident years later when my two children were the same age. I had taken them back to Louisville to show them the path that I took, clarifying that I did not ever want them to do anything similar! But in the course of that visit, it occurred to me that my children at age three were incapable of doing what I had done; they could never have made that ride without getting lost, and this insight really made me think about my own self-image at this time in my life.

I really remember that I believed taking off on the tractor was a safe thing for me to do. I felt this presence with me that I could not explain at that time but made better sense to me later on in my life. In physical terms, I was a three-year-old, but my spirit was older. I felt things differently than the rest of my friends on the block. I saw things from a different vantage point. There was no fear. Instead, I saw things through a lens of joy and curiosity.

As I got older and faced the challenges of the teenage years and adulthood, joy became more elusive, and I found myself returning to the memories of this early period of my life. What I learned from my three-year-old years was that I was truly "in joy." I "en-joyed" every moment, except those moments when I was being spanked (which occurred often). In some ways, the joy was spanked out of me.

Today, I find that space of utter joy still eludes me, but I have so much to be thankful for. I find that when I let my "inner child" emerge, I am immediately transported to that three-year-old spirit. There is joy for me in my work of helping others through my training and consulting and in my books. There is the joy of being married to my soul mate, Susan, and being the proud father of my two wonderful children.

But something else remains for me to find to access that joy, and what I'm searching for is a more constant connection with my divinity. I am searching for a way to be in conscious connection with my Spirit in each and every moment. I believe this union is something that, deep down, we are all seeking, whether we realize it or not.

Finding and sustaining our divine connection is our purpose in life. One of the ways that I establish this inner connection is to embrace joy in what I am doing in the present moment. Doing so is a challenge for me, but a challenge that I approach with joy. More and more each day, I come to realize that, by embracing joy, I see the sacred in life!

- - - - - - - - - - - - - - -

David D. Dameron

I have noticed that, when I am in connection with my divinity, whatever I desire happens. Opportunities increase and doors I needed to open to me do so. Unexpected surprises occur. As I learn how to better attune myself to being happy and joyful and finding fulfillment in what I do, my energy level increases, creating more and more synchronistic events in my life.

My Thoughts—

"A merry heart doeth good like a medicine."

—Proverbs 17:22

Happiness and joy are interconnected. In fact, there is a science to happiness. Studies have proven that happy people are less self-focused, less hostile and abusive, and less vulnerable to diseases. People who are happy and joyful tend to be more loving, forgiving, trusting, sociable, helpful, energetic, and creative. So where can one find happiness and joy? One of the places they can find it is in the present moment! Remember that happiness and joy are an attitude, and we can choose in each moment what we wish our focus to be. It is in the present that we find the sacred in life.

My Thoughts—

"There is no duty we so much underrated as the duty of being happy."

—Robert Louis Stevenson

David D. Dameron

Ancient philosophers believed that happiness and joy were the result of a life of intelligent reflection. I try to help my clients understand that in meditation and quiet reflection or contemplation, they can begin to enhance the power of being present and in the moment. And in the present, we have the opportunity to connect with our divinity. This connection is worth working toward, as it brings a wonderful sense of joy. This morning I practiced meditation for a few moments and practiced being totally present. What did I feel after doing this? What impressions did I receive? How can I be more present throughout the entire day?

My Thoughts—

"No matter how dull, or how mean, or how wise a man is, he feels that happiness is his indisputable right."

—Helen Keller

I write about the topic of divine inheritance often because I have found that I feel joyful when I think about it. When we were given free will, Spirit gave up its life for us. Like someone dying who leaves behind their inheritance, Spirit left us its free will and the ability to choose the life we desire. Through Spirit, what we desire is freely given to us—it is and has always been available to us if we can just envision what we want and believe that we deserve it. Can you identify specific things that are part of your divine inheritance? Some of the things I have identified are perfect health, unlimited abundance, and peace of mind. Like other things, none of these desires could manifest for me until I claimed them. This means claiming them with my heart and attitude, with my words and thoughts, and with my actions.

My Thoughts—

"The soul is filled with love (of God), bound with the bonds of love in great joy."

—Eleazar Ben Judah of Worms

David D. Dameron

When I am able to help my friends and clients—when I connect them to resources that meet their needs—I feel total joy. The client I am working with today is a wonderful spirit and will make a great school principal one day. I arranged for her to call my wife, who is a school principal and who will be a great mentor for her. My client is appreciative of my efforts, and my spirit is rewarded with joy.

My Thoughts—

"We all live with the objective of being happy; our lives are all different and yet the same."

—Anne Frank

When I think about the times when I was most joyful, often I find myself reliving childhood memories. I remember playing all day in the forests behind my house. I remember camping out with my friends in our backyard, as well as fishing all day in the creek just down the road from us. I remember playing our football and baseball games in the corner lot at the end of the street. These were wonderful times for me. I had no worries and I was always full of anticipation of what the next day would bring. Now that I'm an adult, I find myself searching for that same spirit I had as a young boy. What joyful memories do you have from the time when you were young? As you grew older, did you lose that joyful enthusiasm you had for life as a kid? If so, why?

My Thoughts—

"Dance, my heart! Dance
today with joy."

—Kabir

David D. Dameron

I think it is time for all of us to begin celebrating what is right with the world. I would love to produce a newspaper or a television or radio show that features things that are happening in the world that are positive. From time to time, I hear wonderful stories about people overcoming adversity and how they did so. I read about someone who has performed a wonderful act of kindness by helping a person in need. I hear about a new invention or something that improves the quality of life for a number of people. These stories are a source of joy—why are we not writing about them more often and celebrating them? I believe we all can learn from one another, but I am saddened that most of our current media's focus is primarily on the negative aspects and actions of our society.

My Thoughts—

"Joy, beautiful spark of the gods! . . . All people become brothers where you abide."

—Friedrich Schiller

I have noticed that on days when I do not feel motivated or enthusiastic, my "joy quotient" is not present. My thoughts are unfocused. I am usually thinking about something that has happened in the past, or I am focusing on something that has not happened and may never happen. Often, such thoughts are not positive. When I have an attitude of joy, I am much more focused, inspired, and present. I have discovered that joy is a state of mind—or a state of Spirit. What can I do to approach my days more consistently in joy?

My Thoughts—

"I find my joy of living in the fierce and ruthless battles of life, and my pleasure comes from learning something."

—August Strindberg

David D. Dameron

My close friends know that I often look for the spiritual themes in movies and use those themes to illustrate ways we can improve our lives. I have been asked many times what movies I recommend (and there are many) and which movies inspire me. Here are a few that make me feel joyful, make me laugh, and touch my heart. I've included a few short comments after each.

The Shawshank Redemption: There is always hope!
Being There: Life is a state of mind.
Field of Dreams: Build it and He will come.
A Beautiful Mind: True love perseveres over all challenges.
Always: Never hold back love.
Gandhi: Peace is possible.
L.A. Story: Pay attention to signs!
Serendipity: Faith and fate.
Dragonfly: The veil between life and death is very thin.
Harvey: Rabbits are good luck!
Somewhere in Time: The power of intention.
Michael: Angels come in all forms.
Pleasantville: Love transforms everything.

My Thoughts—

"When your life is filled with the desire to see the holiness in everyday life, something magical happens."

—Rabbi Harold Kushner

Thumbing through a catalog of various books and products, I realized how excited I am about life. There is so much to learn and explore. In fact, the feeling I have sometimes is that I want forty hours in a day. I am never bored. Every moment is an opportunity to discover and learn something new. The adventure of life is such a joy for me. I am so blessed and grateful for this experience and to be alive and conscious of my divinity.

My Thoughts—

"Happy is he who has overcome his ego; happy is he who has attained peace; happy is he who has found the truth."

—Buddha

David D. Dameron

The enemy of our spirit is anything that steals energy from us or robs us of our vitality and joy. I realized that to be in joy is to realize that joy is a cause and not an effect. Joy begins with my attitude. It influences my choice making, or how I perceive and react to situations. What actions can I take to allow myself to be more joyful? For example, I feel joy when I express gratitude. I feel joy when I help someone. Conversely, inactivity is an enemy of my spirit; when I become sluggish, whether in my thinking or physically, then I know my spirit does not feel joyful.

My Thoughts—

"What is enthusiasm? It is finding joy in what is wholesome."

—Shan T. Deva

What have been your most joyous moments in life? Write these memories down and, when you find yourself out of connection with Spirit, use them as reminders. Review them every day as part of your morning routine. Use them as ways to bring your thinking into the moment and feel the joy of the memory. Joy transmutes any negative energy or challenge. When you are feeling joy, reflect upon how your life feels at that very moment. Welcome to the home of your divine spirit!

My Thoughts—

"Every day is my best day. This is my life; I'm not going to have this moment again."

—Bernie Siegel

CHAPTER SEVEN:

PEACE

"Being peace doesn't mean simply giving in or giving up or always 'making nice.' It has far more to do with balance, courage, thoughtful action, stillness, self-assessment, preparedness, and patience. It must include compassion, clarity, creativity, and forthrightness as well as justice and wisdom."

—Lenedra J. Carroll,
The Architecture of All Abundance

There is an old saying that "actions speak louder than words." No one embodies this truth more than former President Jimmy Carter. Here is a man who is passionate for peace, has put his passions into action, and has shown the entire world a way to find peaceful solutions to very challenging problems.

One of the vehicles that Jimmy Carter utilizes to promote peace in the world is the Carter Center. Founded in the early eighties by him and his wife, Rosalynn, and in partnership with Emory University in Atlanta, the Carter Center has become one of the most praised non-governmental agencies in the world.

The guiding principles of the Carter Center are a commitment to human rights, reduction of human suffering, seeking peaceful solutions to conflict, enhancing freedom and democracy, and improving the health of people throughout the world.

The Carter Center emphasizes actions and results based on careful research and timely action on critical world issues. The Center is nonpartisan in its actions and is known to collaborate with private and public organizations in accomplishing its mission.

In my research on the accomplishments of the Carter Center, the list was quite extensive. Here is just a sampling of the Center's accomplishments:

- The Center has spearheaded a global effort to reduce cases of Guinea worm disease.
- Jimmy Carter has traveled to Venezuela to work with opposition groups that have been embroiled in violent disagreements.
- The Carter Center has overseen parliamentary elections in Jamaica.
- The Rosalynn Carter Georgia Mental Health Forum has been instrumental in establishing performance measures to improve the state's mental services.
- The Carter Center sought to influence and improve Nigeria's electoral procedures and processes.

In recognition of his work for peace, and in recognition of its effectiveness, Jimmy Carter was awarded the Nobel Peace Prize in Oslo, Norway, on December 10, 2002. He was lauded for his decades of tireless effort to find peaceful solutions to international conflicts, to advance democracy and human rights, and to promote economic and social development.

Besides being a noted author, an ambassador of peace, and a human rights activist, Jimmy Carter is also known for his involvement with Habitat for Humanity. This project was designed to battle against poverty and provide deserving families with a means to own their homes, and give them access to a higher quality of life.

- - - - - - - - - - - - - -

This chapter is about *peace*. I selected former President Jimmy Carter, among many excellent examples, as an individual whose actions and approach to life are built around a reverence for peace. Why is Jimmy Carter so successful at promoting peace in the world, so much so that he was awarded the Nobel Peace Prize? He brings peace to the world because he has found peace within his own soul.

I believe that peace is at the core of our divine inheritance. It is our basic nature, contrary to what you might believe from witnessing what is happening on this planet at this time. And it's true that history would seem to illustrate that the human race is intrinsically violent, with no regard for human life or other forms of life.

But war and violence on this planet are just the outward manifestations of what is occurring within each of us. We resort to violence on a personal level as well as on a world scale; that's why you will also encounter violence based on fear at work, misuse of power, and people's desire and need to exert control.

There will be peace on this planet when the majority of the world's population decides to live in peace, and that will come about when people have found peace within themselves, as has Jimmy Carter. When people have found their divine connection, they will know that we are all interconnected on this planet, to each other and to the earth itself.

We may look different from each other, belonging to different races, worshipping in different ways, and with different likes and dislikes; but when we all embrace peace, we will feel a mutual respect for each other that transcends those differences. With peace at the center of our hearts and actions, we will reach compromises over different viewpoints and seek collaboration over competition.

For there to be peace in the world we must find that peace, that sacred place, inside ourselves. And when we do, our actions and our words will become representative of the peace we feel inside, as Jimmy Carter's actions and words are an outward manifestation of his inner self.

The day is coming where there will be peace on earth. It is our destiny. True, we may have to endure even more pain and suffering before we realize that destiny; but rest assured that peace is part of our divine birthright and our divine inheritance. Like anything in life, though, in order to have it, you have to claim it! That is the choice that each of us must decide to take; so I invite you to claim it for yourself, right now, and in each present moment to come. Then you will see the sacred in life!

- - - - - - - - - - - - - -

David D. Dameron

I saw the actor Martin Sheen interviewed on television, and he made a wonderful statement that embodied the nature of peace. He said, "We don't go to heaven. We become heaven." His statement reminded me that life is in a process of "becoming." We are all evolving, and our humanity is slowly catching up to our divinity. When the day comes—and it will—that we merge our divinity and our humanity, then peace will reign on this planet, because peace will reign in our hearts. It is in this special place that we will have peace in the world because we will see the sacred in life.

My Thoughts—

"Blessed are the peacemakers, for they shall be called the children of God."

—Matthew 5:9

I am often asked whether I truly believe that peace will someday come to this world. Many look at our world as being violent, and certainly that appears to be true. But the exterior world is only a reflection of what is being expressed from inside each of us. When peace is present in our hearts, there you will find love, patience, kindness, and compassion. Where you find peace in the world is where you find people who are at peace with their spirit. How can I find peace of mind within myself?

My Thoughts—

"Seek to be in harmony
with all your neighbors
… live in peace with
your brethren."

—Confucianism

David D. Dameron

By spiritual law, every thought on which we focus and concentrate is sent out into the world and returns to us. Every feeling we have in our heart is also sent out into the world and returns to us, as is every word we speak. If we wish to live a happy, fulfilled, and divinely led life, does it not make sense that our thoughts, feelings, words, and actions should embody peace? When we are present and our focus is on peace, then our world is a reflection of that peace.

My Thoughts—

"There is no happiness
greater than peace."

—Buddhism

When do I feel most in connection with my spirit? I would answer, "When I am at peace with my thoughts, my feelings, and with myself." When I hold my thoughts in the present, I feel great love and compassion in my heart. In this space of the present moment, I hear clearly the voice of my spirit, and this divine presence assures me that I am never alone. In this sacred space, I imagine my vision for the world and my life. I know that, if I can envision something, then it has already begun to manifest in my life. Whether my thoughts are about my desire for peace on earth, or about something else I desire, by thinking and envisioning what I want, I am merely claiming what has already been given.

My Thoughts—

"Without meditation, where is peace? Without peace, where is happiness?"

—Hinduism

David D. Dameron

If you want to experience peace, give up conflict. If you want to embrace love, then give up hate. If you want to be in perfect health, then see yourself as being whole, and develop habits that support that wholeness. If you want to embrace your divinity, then act as if you are an aspect of the Divine. Everything you desire in your life is brought to you by the choices you make. In this very moment, every thought, word, feeling, and action is a reflection of your focus. Are your thoughts of peace, and if not, why not? Are you willing to change your thinking to receive the gift of peace?

My Thoughts—

"God will guide men to peace. If they will heed Him, He will lead them from the darkness of war to the light of peace."

—Islam

In the past, certain relationships in my life were a source of conflict; but recently, I have noticed that relationships with people with whom I previously experienced conflict have changed for the better. In examining this change, I noticed that I no longer feel angry with these people. At some point, without knowing it, I forgave them—or perhaps they are a reflection of a change that occurred within me. I am reminded that when we look at others and the world, we see only a reflection of what we ourselves are inside. I like the idea that I am doing my small part to bring peace to this planet by bringing peace to my heart.

My Thoughts—

"The wise esteem peace and quiet above all else."

—Taoism

David D. Dameron

I did not feel peaceful today, and my outer world reflected that lack of peace back to me. A client missed her appointment with me, and that upset me. Additionally, I did not do my morning routine and I felt sluggish, unmotivated, and emotionally reactive all day. I found myself in an emotional space that I did not like, unable to be in the moment or to feel peaceful. How could I have approached my day differently so I could connect with peace within myself and manifest that peace?

My Thoughts—

"When a man's ways please the Lord he maketh even his enemies to be at peace with him."

—Judaism

I support certain organizations whose stated mission is to bring peace to this planet by political, social, educational, or environmental means. Their intent inspired me to support them. I am sometimes asked what groups I support; here is a short list of national groups I have supported in the past:

- Doctors Without Borders
- American Red Cross
- Amnesty International
- Glide Foundation
- Public Citizen
- Disabled American Veterans
- The Carter Center
- International Campaign For Tibet
- The Nature Conservancy
- Native American Rights Fund
- National Public Radio
- Institute of Heartmath

This support is one way I reflect the peace I feel within myself and manifest that peace into my world.

My Thoughts—

"All men should live in
peace with their fellows.
This is the Lord's
desire."

—Jainism

David D. Dameron

Creative visualization is a wonderful technique I utilize to help me achieve a state of inner peace. I invite you to try it, too. Find a comfortable chair in a private place and sit for a few minutes with your eyes closed, just concentrating on your breathing and trying not to be distracted by any thoughts. At some point, when you have begun to feel peaceful and quiet, imagine you are on a tropical beach, sitting in a beach chair under the shade of a palm tree, with your feet in the sand. The wind is gently blowing in your face, and you are listening to the waves rolling onto the beach. The temperature is perfect. You are in total bliss. Welcome to peace. Peace is our normal and natural state of being, if we can learn to embrace it in our hectic days. Daily, or especially when you are feeling stressed, try this technique.

My Thoughts—

"Let the earth be free from trouble and men live at peace under the protection of the Divine."

—Shinto

I am often asked how one can attain a state of peace and maintain it throughout the day. I realize this is hard to do, especially if we are easily influenced and reactive to things happening around us. To attain and maintain true inner peace, we need to heal the split between our personality/ego and our divinity. We must learn how to become detached emotionally from outcomes or expectations. We must give up trying to control people and situations. We must recognize our fears and tame them. What steps can I take to bring more peace into my life?

My Thoughts—

"War is death, while peace is life."

—Bahai

CHAPTER EIGHT:

WELLNESS

"So unconscious has humanity become of the source of its helpfulness, and so closed are the avenues through which such aid may come, that many people are almost defeated by their environment, the pressure being so great that enforced duty carries them far beyond the natural limit. One should never be called upon to sacrifice physical, mental or spiritual welfare through the performance of duties."

—Thurman Fleet, *Rays of the Dawn*

Over the years I have benefited from stories from individuals who have overcome tremendous adversities. One of my spiritual teachers, whom I will call Caroline in this story in order to honor her privacy, has overcome tremendous health challenges during the course of her life. I found her story to be an inspiration.

In 1977, while at a seminar, Caroline fainted and was hospitalized for extensive diagnostic tests. Her colleagues had thought that she might be suffering from fatigue.

When Caroline returned to her office the head nurse at her company told her to see an internist for a diagnosis and said she could not return to work without a note of permission from a doctor. After the internist saw Caroline, he referred her to several specialists.

After seeing several doctors, something Caroline had not expected at all changed her life dramatically. A neurosurgeon she had seen wrote a note to her company stating that Caroline was totally disabled and could no longer do any kind of work.

The neurosurgeon had concluded that Caroline had irreversible, cervical and lumbar osteoarthritis with the possibility of herniated discs. Additionally, an otolaryngologist found that she had benign positional vertigo, a gastroenterologist diagnosed esophageal reflux, and a neurologist suspected that Caroline had been exposed to some environmental toxins at work. It seemed a number of challenges she had overcome when younger were now causing serious health problems.

Her physicians found evidence of lasting effects from Caroline's bout with smallpox at the age of one month and possible damage from having been overcome by carbon monoxide fumes when she was fourteen due to a faulty floor furnace. The carbon monoxide poisoning had been a near-death experience for her, and for years afterward she had severe respiratory difficulties. Lastly, Caroline had contracted encephalomyelitis (inflammation of the brain and the spinal cord) when she was twenty-one, and that had left her with even more health problems.

As you might expect, Caroline's employer placed her on long-term disability. To compound the stress of such a major change in her life and her physical challenges, these changes came at a time when she was undergoing grief therapy with a psychiatrist to cope with the death of five people to whom she had been very close throughout her life, all of whom had died within the previous eighteen months.

Can you imagine trying to cope with such radical changes and challenges? And can you imagine that something as simple as the gift of a book could be the means by which you could find relief and renewed hope? Well, read on.

In February of 1978, one month before Caroline's fiftieth birthday, her son visited her and brought her a gift. He came into her bedroom, where his mother was temporarily confined by the straps of a cervical-lumbar traction device.

Underneath his arm, he was carrying a book on hatha yoga. He stayed long enough to urge his mother, strongly, to take up the practice of yoga. Then he set the book by her bedside, wished her well, and left to go home.

Caroline began to thumb through the book, telling herself over and over that she would never be able to do the poses illustrated. Furthermore, her neurologist had warned her that she must avoid getting up and down from the floor, or risk further injury.

So Caroline read through the book, skipping the chapters on the yoga poses; but she became intrigued by the articles on nutrition and breathing practices (pranayama). Caroline decided that she could at least work on improving her diet and increasing her breathing capacity.

She began to work diligently at changing her nutritional habits and her breathing, and almost immediately she experienced a significant and unmistakable energy increase. For the first time in years, she began to experience a sense of well-being.

She then began to do simple yoga poses and gentle stretching. Her results were remarkable; within a few months, she was practicing a full routine of yoga, with significant improvement in her physical, mental, and emotional well-being, and no ill effects. After eighteen months of practice, she was achieving more advanced yoga postures, including warrior poses and even head stands.

Having taken control of her wellness through the art of yoga and nutrition, Caroline opened a yoga center in 1980 and has been teaching hatha yoga to hundreds of students since. She and her story are testaments to the blessings of wellness.

- - - - - - - - - - - - - - -

Caroline's story inspired me to reflect on my own well-being; I think it serves to encourage all of us to be grateful for whatever level of well-being we are experiencing now. This chapter is about *wellness*, and it is important to understand what wellness really means.

Most of us only think of wellness in connection with our physical health, and certainly that is an important aspect of being well. But true wellness encompasses much more. We are holistic creatures, which means that we are multifaceted in nature. In addition to our physical health, our well-being is dependent on our spiritual, mental, and emotional health.

Holistic means to be whole; to be whole, to be balanced, all facets of our natures must be functioning well. A relationship with our spirit is necessary to forge a connection with our divinity. A healthy mental outlook lets us perceive the world positively and attract positive energy to ourselves and our lives.

Our emotional natures are also a factor in determining whether we approach life positively, with passion and feeling, or less positively, with depression and anxiety. Finally, the health of our physical bodies determines our ability to have the energy and the mobility to meet daily challenges.

The good news is that we can take control of our lives and make positive changes in all of these areas. Addressing only one area will probably bring only limited success, but through proper habits that address all four areas—spiritual, mental, emotional, and physical—we can live a life of joy, filled with well-being. That's what Caroline chose to do.

Through the blessing of her son's encouragement, Caroline decided to take control of her wellness. As she did, she released the true spirit of healing that waited inside her. I wish I could put into words how powerful our thoughts and feelings are. When we can tap into our spiritual natures and the power for change that resides there, all things become possible.

I do not dismiss the importance of physicians in the process to find true wellness; but modern medicine deals with effects rather than causes and it focuses on the physical. Behind every physical disease is a spiritual cause. Heal yourself in spirit and you will heal yourself physically. That understanding was the true gift of Caroline's story for me, and I hope for you as well.

- - - - - - - - - - - - - - -

David D. Dameron

I have been feeling unconnected to my work and to the writing of my book, and feeling as gloomy as the rainy weather outside; so I asked in my morning meditation what I needed to do to get past this feeling of stagnation in my life. The answer that came to me was to take better care of my body. I received the message that I should focus on healthy eating and exercise, to purify my system of toxins. From my meditation, I came to realize that when my personality feels toxic, it might be the result of feeling toxic physically. That relationship is what science refers to as the *mind-body connection*.

My Thoughts—

"Our prayers should be for a sound mind in a healthy body."

—Juvenal, *Satires*

After much urging from my doctor, I finally gave in and had a colonoscopy procedure. My doctor had been reiterating that I am over fifty and at risk, and reminded me that my father had colon cancer. I am truly appalled at the negative messages doctors feel they must emphasize. My inner guidance in this matter has always been that everything is fine with my colon, and that doing the procedure would only reinforce what I already know. As it turned out, the procedure confirmed that approach—everything was fine. In the future, I plan to ask Spirit to guide me as to whether I should have a medical procedure. And rather than act from fear, I plan to rely on the power of positive suggestion, which can be of tremendous benefit. Daily, I affirm that "I am perfect health."

My Thoughts—

"I feel no care of coin;
Well-doing is my wealth;
My mind to me an
empire is, While grace
affordeth health."

—Robert Southwell

David D. Dameron

When I am seeking balance and wellness in my life, I engage in a forty-day process developed and described by author John Randolph Price in his book *The Abundance Book*. He refers to the plan as the forty-day prosperity plan, but the plan is more about connecting with the source of our abundance than with prosperity. I have found his technique to be invaluable in changing my attitude when I am moody or worried. Through working with this plan, I have seen that wellness in my life springs not only from the health of my body, but is connected to my thoughts and my relationship with God as well.

My Thoughts—

"Better to hunt in fields
for health unbrought,
than fee the doctor for a
nauseous draught."

—John Dryden

Living in wellness is about practicing self-care. I have told my clients that all of our problems and worries can be traced to two things. One is our relationship with our spirit. The second is how we feel about our self. When I do not feel positive about my life, I go to these two areas and examine whether I am connected with God and Spirit, and how I am feeling about myself. For the next few days, each day, I record something I love about myself in my journal and I make it a point to do something for myself each day. Soon I feel connected with Spirit again and feel good about myself. What specific things can you do to improve your relationship with Spirit and with yourself?

My Thoughts—

"Say you are well,
or all is well with you,
and God shall hear your
words
and make them true."

—Anonymous

David D. Dameron

Did you know that there is a connection between laughter and wellness? I attended a workshop on using humor as a tool in training, and the speaker opened with this illustration:

"Consider the following description of a physical reaction: The neural circuits in your brain begin to reverberate. Chemical and electrical impulses start flowing rapidly through your body. The pituitary gland is stimulated; hormones and endorphins race through your blood. Your body temperature rises half a degree, your pulse rate and blood pressure increase, your arteries and thoracic muscles contract, your vocal chords quiver, and your face contorts. Pressure builds in your lungs. Your lower jaw suddenly becomes uncontrollable, and breath bursts from your mouth at nearly seventy miles an hour."

The speaker was relating the clinical description of laughter. There are times when I know, without a shred of doubt, that I am connected to my spirit, and those times are inevitably when I am laughing. What can I do to find more humor in my life?

My Thoughts—

"I have good health, good thoughts, and good humour, thanks be to God almighty."

—William Byrd

I loved life when I was three years old, but I can imagine that my mom probably wished I did not love life quite so much. She had her hands full with me. One day I accompanied her to the local pharmacy, carrying a bag of my old toys. She let me bring them, thinking I'd just leave them in the car, but I managed to sneak them into the store with me. While she was engaged with the storekeeper, I took them out of the bag and put them on the shelf where the new toys were. I then replaced the old toys in my bag with new toys and tried to walk out of the store. The manager stopped me as he had witnessed this whole affair. I remember him laughing about it. My mother, however, did not find it so amusing, and once we got home, the way my rear end felt kept me from finding it amusing either. But I do find it very amusing now, and I still laugh about this episode every time I think about it.

My Thoughts—

"One morning I shot an elephant in my pajamas. How he got into my pajamas I'll never know."

—Groucho Marx

David D. Dameron

My family still loves to tell the story of the night I saw the story of Peter Pan on television. As my family watched me, I climbed up on the ledge of our fireplace and announced to everyone that I *was* Peter Pan. I then proceeded to dive off head first, thinking I was going to be able to fly like Peter Pan. My family was stunned, and so was I. I lay on the floor, crying, with a huge knot on my forehead. My family was convinced from that moment on that there was something wrong with me. What memories do you have that can bring humor to your day?

My Thoughts—

"Everything is funny, as long as it's happening to somebody else."

—Will Rogers

A good friend told me a story about an elderly couple that lived in her apartment complex. The husband was close to death and he had decided to die in his home with assistance from hospice workers. Sitting beside him, his wife noticed that he wanted to say something to her. She took his hand as he looked into her eyes and said to her, "What's wrong dear?" She responded, "I wanna hold your hand." He then responded, "The Beatles." And then he died. This is a true story. This gentleman had always been known for his humor, and even with his final breath, he chose to leave this life in peace and with humor. This was a person who understood wellness and timing in the moment!

My Thoughts—

"Total absence of humour renders life impossible."

—Colette

David D. Dameron

When my clients express a desire to make positive changes in their lives, I recommend that they sit down with a piece of paper and pen in privacy. On this piece of paper, I urge them to write a wellness statement. If you would like to see positive changes in your own life, you can do the same. Spiritually, physically, emotionally, socially, and intellectually, how do you envision your ideal life? How do you see your relationship with God? With your friends? With yourself? Your career? Are you living your highest truth? Once you finish, I suggest you review your wellness statement periodically. Where are you out of balance? What actions can you take to accomplish the goals and desires of your wellness statement?

My Thoughts—

"The path of duty lies in what is near, and man seeks for it in what is remote."

—Mencius

You can enhance the quality of wellness in your life by taking specific actions. Commit to practicing better self-care. Set up a support system that mirrors your intentions in life. Take workshops, read, get a massage, find a hobby, do something creative, and surround yourself with people who support the type of life you wish to live. It is not selfish to take care of your needs. In reality, when you take care of yourself, you are a better person to the people who are important in your life. What specific things can you do to practice better self-care? When, specifically, are you going to take these steps?

My Thoughts—

"Man is wise . . . when
he recognizes no greater
enemy than himself."

—Marguerite of Navarre

David D. Dameron

    I write often that our bodies and our thoughts are frequencies of energy. The more positive we are, the higher our frequency. When we are negative and moody, our frequency drops to a lower level. A wonderful technique for raising our frequency is the practice of toning and chanting. Whenever we hum or sing an inspirational song, we raise the frequency of our body and our thoughts. Chanting has been practiced for thousands of years in the eastern part of the world, and this mystical practice now has become accepted in the Western world, just as meditation has. Science is now researching the positive benefits of toning and chanting on our physiology.

My Thoughts—

"The melting voice
through mazes running;
untwisting all the chains
that tie the hidden soul
of harmony."

—John Milton

Our mind is probably the greatest pharmacy in the world. Research is showing that our emotions and the quality of our thoughts affect our DNA structure and every cell in our body. To put it simply, if you think *cancer* you can actually create cancer in your body. It is time for all of us to pay closer attention to the quality of our thoughts and our environments. Does it not make sense that if we surround ourselves with positive thoughts and things in our lives, then we will promote a positive environment outside of ourselves? In terms of our internal biology, does it not make sense that cells respond to the messages they receive, both positive and negative?

My Thoughts—

"Man is made by his belief. As he believes, so he is."

—*The Bhagavad-Gita*

David D. Dameron

When I practice meditation or creative visualization, my purpose is not to make something specific happen. Instead, meditation and creative visualization are methods by which we can go within to tap into a higher vibration—the vibration of our spirit. When we access these higher states, amazing things start to happen in our lives and in our world. Meditation and creative visualization connect us with Spirit, and help us stay in the present moment. True wellness is measured by the quality of our connection with our spirit, and this sacred connection is found only in the moment. Keeping our focus on the present is our most challenging spiritual barrier, and it is also the source of our greatest spiritual advancement. When we do find and maintain this focus, then we will see the sacred in life.

My Thoughts—

"The wise, who knows that one hidden in the cave of the heart as God, is liberated from the fetters of joy and sorrow."

—*The Upanishads*

172

CHAPTER NINE:

CREATIVITY

"Human nature does not have to be changed to eliminate war on the planet for all time. It is human unconscious programming that has to be changed, which is totally feasible."

—Willis Harmon, Ph.D., and Howard Rheingold,
Higher Creativity

A few weeks ago, when I was working on the outline for this book, I knew I wanted to write a chapter on the subject of *creativity*. After I went through my files of stories, I decided I wanted to write about an episode I had seen on a television show called *Dharma and Greg*.

This romantic comedy follows the lives of two characters. Dharma is a free-spirited yoga teacher, and Greg is an open-minded, Harvard-educated attorney. This couple fell in love at first sight, and they ended up getting married after their first date. Obviously, part of my own attraction to the show was the parallel to the story of how my wife and I came together, a story I related in the introduction to this book.

Though I knew I wanted to write about that episode, I needed to see it again. The show is currently in syndication, and I knew it would be a challenge to find the episode.

My first avenue was to talk to my daughter. She lifeguards during the summer at a country club here in San Antonio, and last summer she met Thomas Gibson, the actor who plays Greg on the television show. Apparently, he has a house in San Antonio. My plan was that, when my daughter saw Thomas Gibson again at the pool, she could ask him how I might find a tape of the program; but unfortunately Thomas Gibson didn't make an appearance at the pool again this summer.

So I decided to search the Internet, specifically Amazon.com. As I searched for episodes of *Dharma and Greg*, I discovered that the show had not yet been put onto DVD or VHS.

I continued my search on the Internet and found several *Dharma and Greg* websites. Still, I could not uncover any episodes on tape. I finally did find the name of the episode I was looking for, "Yes, We have No Bananas (Or Anything Else for That Matter)." Having the title was a start, but what I really needed to remember was what actually happened in the episode so I could write about it.

Suddenly, as I was about to log off of the Internet, a box from eBay dropped down on my computer screen. It listed three items for sale on eBay that were related to the *Dharma and Greg* television show. One item was a hat; another was a poster; and, on seeing the third item, I practically fell out of my chair. It was the script to an episode that the seller just labeled "Bananas"!

It was the script of the episode that I was searching for. The problem was that I had only ten minutes left to bid on this item. I desperately tried to get into my eBay account, but I had not used it for two or three years and had forgotten my password.

I watched helplessly as my item disappeared from the bidding list. I went ahead and asked eBay for my password and, without much hope, requested that I be notified for the next thirty days on any items for sale related to the *Dharma and Greg* television show.

A day or so later, I was retrieving my e-mails and opened an e-mail from eBay on some *Dharma and Greg* items. When I went to eBay, I couldn't believe my eyes; the "Bananas" script was up for bid again! Apparently, the previous bidder had backed out for some reason.

I put a bid in for the script, learned that I had won the bid a week later, and within two more days I received the script in the mail. And that's why I'm now able to relate to you the events of that episode, which are a great example of the power of creativity.

- - - - - - - - - - - - - -

During the show, Dharma takes Greg downtown to show him a building she's rented next to a bus stop. When Greg asks Dharma what she is going to do with the store, she answers that she's going to sell something, but she doesn't know what.

Of course, this leads to other questions from Greg about why she leased a store when she had no idea what she was going to sell. Her answer is the same each time: that it didn't matter, because the building and location would be perfect for anything.

Dharma's parents arrive with some old tables and chairs, and they begin helping Dharma paint the store. As they are fixing up the place, a man walks into the store and asks Dharma what she is going to sell. Her response is, "What do you need?"

The man asks if he can sit down until the bus comes, which Dharma gladly allows him to do. Soon the entire store is filled with people waiting for the bus. When someone wants a newspaper, someone else in the store lends them theirs, and the people begin to help each other out, exchanging food and even lending each other cell phones.

People are chatting, eating bag lunches, reading, and even playing backgammon. About this time, the city inspector shows up, wanting to know where Dharma's license is for selling goods. If, by now, you've learned anything about Dharma and her approach to business, you won't be surprised that Dharma is utterly sincere when she tells the inspector that she is not selling anything.

When Greg comes by, to his surprise he sees the store is full of people. Trying to understand what is happening, he sits down with an airline pilot, who begins sharing little bottles of liquor with him. Several bottles of liquor later, Greg looks up at his wife with a smile on his face and says, "Nice place you have here."

A few nights later, Greg comes home to his wife to find coffee cups all over the apartment. Dharma informs him that Starbucks liked her building and were so impressed with the number of people she had attracted that the company offered her ten thousand dollars and all the coffee she could drink for the rest of her life if she sold her business to them.

Needless to say, Dharma said yes. Her husband Greg was left shaking his head.

- - - - - - - - - - - - - -

As you can see, what started out as a search for an episode had two stories interwoven. The first is the story of how I found the script, and the second is the story itself. Creativity is about tapping into our divinity where anything we need resides. And here is how it works.

I set in motion an idea, and look how the universe responded. All I needed to do was to pay attention and be patient and know that by holding my intention in my consciousness, sooner or later what I desired would manifest.

The episode itself is rich in symbolism and meaning. Dharma wanted to start something, but did not know what. So she created a space for something to happen and just let it unfold.

Greg struggled with this approach because his orientation to the world is quite different. As Dharma pointed out during the episode, Greg needed external validation for him to become comfortable with an idea.

Dharma did not. She followed her inner guidance, took a risk, went with the flow, and look what happened. This mindset is the essence of creativity. We are all creative, and because we are divine beings, we can create anything we desire.

The key to success through creativity is to employ your creativity constantly and to know, without a doubt, that you are drawing upon the creative juices of the universe when you do so. Nothing is held back from us if we believe in our heart of hearts that *anything* is possible.

Finally, as you read the following passages, please note that the quotes at the bottom are representative of individuals who did not have the foresight to understand the creative process. As you will understand by reading the quotes, there is no limit to what is possible when it comes to understanding the power of creativity. There are no challenges for which there are no creative solutions. Understanding the source of our creativity

David D. Dameron

opens up great possibilities for humanity. It opens up an avenue by which we can see the sacred in life.

- - - - - - - - - - - - - - -

When I am out of connection with my divinity, that is the time, without a doubt, for me to focus on being creative. Whether I am working on my book, composing music, or designing a project, I find that when I am creative I feel a connection with life. What other opportunities are available for my creativity to emerge? In what areas of my life could I be more creative? How can I tap my creativity today?

My Thoughts—

"There is no reason anyone would want a computer in their home."

—Ken Olson, president, chairman and founder of Digital Equipment Corp., 1977

David D. Dameron

I have found that a person with a vision for his or her life also has a sense of purpose. Through a sense of purpose, life has meaning. I have also discovered that having a sense of purpose fuels my passion and my creativity. I like rediscovering, again and again, that I can make my ideas manifest, whether they are big or small. When you feel a need for more passion in your life, look for ways to become creative. Creativity is our connection with our divinity.

My Thoughts—

"This 'telephone' has too many shortcomings to be seriously considered as a means of communication. The device is inherently of no value to us."

—Western Union internal memo, 1876

My client today talked about her concept of *tapping*. She said that when she feels Spirit is trying to point her in the right direction, she feels a tapping. This tapping is an intuitive feeling for her. In any challenge she faces, she looks for possibilities and she listens to the tapping. Once she is shown the path or decision she should take, she then draws upon her creativity to look for ways to manifest that change in her life.

My Thoughts—

"The concept is interesting and well-formed, but in order to earn better than a 'C,' the idea must be feasible."

—A Yale University management professor in response to Fred Smith's paper proposing reliable overnight delivery service. Smith went on to found Federal Express Corp.

David D. Dameron

I saw an interview on television in which a woman told an amazing story about creativity. She explained that a few years ago she went into a deep depression over the breakup of a long-term relationship with her boyfriend. Seeing that she was down, her friends started sending her cards to cheer her up. Some of the cards were handmade. She was so inspired by her friends' cards and by how much they did to help her get past her depression that she decided to start her own greeting card company. Her cards had a particular focus—they were designed for people facing challenges in their lives, and designed to raise their spirits. The business was tremendously successful—today this woman is a millionaire. She is an example of someone who used her creativity to turn a life challenge into opportunity.

My Thoughts—

"Who the hell wants to
hear actors talk?"

—H. M. Warner, Warner Brothers, 1927

Most people think of creativity as being related to being an artist or a musician, and they feel if they have no musical or artistic talent then creativity has no place in their life. The truth is that we are all creative, no matter what our pursuits. In each moment, we are making choices as we try to understand how to live a happier and more fulfilling life. Since we are divine beings, does it not make sense that we have access to anything we need at any moment? We just have to learn how to ask and how to listen. Our creativity is enhanced when we *pay attention.*

My Thoughts—

"A cookie store is a bad idea. Besides, the market research reports say America likes crispy cookies, not soft and chewy cookies like you make."

—Response to Debbi Fields' idea of starting Mrs. Fields' Cookies

Creativity requires positive energy; it's hard to be creative when you are feeling sluggish, tired, or depressed. Here are some ideas to raise your energy level. As you feel more energy, you can engage in a project with more creativity—and apply your creative energy to your life, too!

- Meditate
- Go for a walk
- Read something inspirational
- Rent a movie that you enjoy and that inspires you
- Listen to a motivational tape
- Dance to your favorite music
- Take a nap
- Play a practical joke (be nice!) on someone
- Laugh
- Do something to help someone

My Thoughts—

"We don't like their sound, and guitar music is on the way out."

—Decca Recording Co., rejecting the Beatles, 1962

Life is about movement. It is about expansion. To be alive is to be motivated and inspired. When you feel disconnected, keep moving, keep creating, and keep expanding. Ask God for help. You are not alone. Once you make a connection and feel the divine current, you will feel the magic and the limitless possibilities; functioning creatively, each day, will help you maintain that connection. Life is a state of mind, and staying creative helps your attitude and your inner connection!

My Thoughts—

"Heavier-than-air flying machines are impossible."

—Lord Kelvin, president, Royal Society, 1895

David D. Dameron

Our creativity knows no boundaries. I was told a story that illustrates this fact: A jazz pianist who had been blind all of his life taught himself to play a player piano. The interesting aspect here was that the player piano was set for two people playing at the same time. The jazz pianist didn't know that and, consequently, he learned to play at the pace of two people. The point here is that his consciousness was unaware of a limitation others took for granted and, being unaware of it, his consciousness was not hampered by that limitation—it did not hold him back. What limitations do you place on yourself that inhibit your creative expression? What might happen if you ignored those limitations and reached for something beyond them?

My Thoughts—

"If I had thought about it, I wouldn't have done the experiment. The literature was full of examples that said you can't do this."

—Spencer Silver on the work that led to the unique adhesives for 3-M "Post-it" Notepads

Whether you are juggling long work hours and personal responsibilities, figuring out how to get the kids to different appointments at the same time, or searching for ways to pay the bills, all of these challenges call for the use of creativity. We are all creative beings by nature. The challenges you face each day all have a possible solution. Each of us has the capacity to be more than what we are. This is our purpose in life—to bring forth our divinity, where our creativity and our potential reside!

My Thoughts—

"Drill for oil? You mean drill into the ground to try and find oil? You're crazy."

—Drillers who Edwin L. Drake tried to enlist to his project to drill for oil in 1859

Have you ever wondered about the source of our creative power? Where do our ideas and insights come from? I have told many of my clients that I have never had an original idea in my life. Nothing I write about is unique. My point is that our ideas and insights have always been in existence because they come from God. Creativity is about finding answers that have already been given and that we discover by turning inward and listening for direction. Fulfillment and peace exist now. When we see the sacred in life, then we can truly *see*, and we will then know how to live our lives in peace.

My Thoughts—

"Everything than can be invented has been invented."

—Charles H. Duell, Commissioner, U.S. Office of Patents, 1899

CHAPTER TEN:

PATIENCE

"Patience is the missing link in the discernment process, in the search for clarity of calling and readiness of heart, and the waiting for events to unfurl and talents to ripen."

—Gregg LeVoy, *Callings*

I wrote in the introduction to this book about the time in my life when I met my wife, Susan. When Susan and I decided to be married, she agreed to move to San Antonio from her home in Michigan, and I took on the task of finding the perfect home for us. I was living in a small apartment at that time, and we knew we would definitely need a larger place since Susan owned her own house in Michigan and had two wonderful dogs.

Throughout the fall of 1999, I looked for a house to rent. We thought renting was our best option until Susan found a job and we were both settled together. During that fall Susan made monthly trips to San Antonio, and the two of us would drive around town, looking for a house.

But fall faded into winter, and we still had found nothing. The houses we looked at were dismal. We were finding that rental homes in the price range we were looking for generally were not well maintained. Susan's house had sold in Michigan even before the real-estate person could put a sign in the yard, and she was now living in a small apartment, with her furniture in storage. We were both on hold—our marriage, our living arrangements, and our desire to be together were utterly stalled.

I was feeling a great deal of pressure. I wanted to find the right place for us, and I knew how important a home environment was going to be to Susan. She was uprooting herself from her family and friends to move to Texas, and I wanted everything to be perfect.

As I was meditating one morning, I was trying to figure out why we could not find a satisfactory rental house. Something was not flowing. There was resistance, and that resistance, I realized, was a clue for me to pay closer attention to the situation.

It finally came to me why we were having this problem: we were meant to buy a house, not rent one. Once this idea occurred to me, I had a strong instinct that I was right, and when I called Susan, she felt the same way. We both knew immediately that buying a house was the course we needed to pursue.

So I called a wonderful real-estate agent and gave her a list of the features we wanted, based on features I'd liked in other houses I'd owned. She immediately located several houses for us to consider, and I began looking at possible houses in December that were similar to others I had owned in San Antonio.

Each day I would call Susan to apprise her of my progress. She made another trip to town and participated in our continued search for a house. But though we both felt we were getting closer to finding the home meant for us, by the end of December we had still found nothing that really called to us. Susan flew back to Michigan, and I continued the search. I was growing impatient!

Our realtor finally found a house that she said perfectly matched our wish list. She was right; I saw the house and was drawn to it immediately. I could see Susan and myself living there, happy that we were together and having a good life. But the seller had specified the house would not be available immediately. Though I liked the house very much, I was also struggling with needing to find something very quickly, before Susan's scheduled move to San Antonio.

I called Susan about the house, and together we decided to offer the owner a contract. I was relieved to have come to a decision, but became concerned when I received the report from the house inspection. The inspector had noted a number of problems I had missed seeing, and, among other concerns, he said the house needed a new roof.

Accordingly, Susan and I put into the final contract that the seller needed to replace the roof, and he declined our offer and refused to negotiate. That evening, I sat down in my apartment feeling totally frustrated.

Then my inner voice reminded me that things were not "flowing." Why, I asked myself, was there so much resistance and so many roadblocks to our purchase of this house? Why had I missed seeing so many of the house's shortcomings when we'd looked at it?

I talked to Susan about it, and she gently reminded me that I needed to let go of worrying about her move to town, relax more, and flow with the process. She said she was confident that, when the time was right, we would find the right house.

As always, I felt better after talking to her. One evening the next week, I found myself driving through the neighborhood where the house we had hoped to buy was located. In addition to liking the house, I was attracted to the part of town it was in and its neighborhood.

A couple of blocks from the house my eye caught a "For Sale" sign, and, looking at the house as I drove by, I felt something "click" inside of me. I turned around and drove by the house again, and the feeling became stronger. I called my real-estate agent as soon as I got back to my apartment, and we set an appointment the next day.

When the agent and I visited the house the next morning, I knew without a doubt that this was the house for Susan and me. Because of my recent experience with the other house, I tried to remain cautious—I felt I had jumped into that situation too quickly and possibly for the wrong reasons. I didn't want to get my hopes up again, only to find there were insurmountable obstacles to buying this house as well. Additionally, this house was unlike houses I'd owned previously, and I had imagined, all along, that the house we purchased would have many things in common with other houses I'd lived in.

But so many things about the house were perfect for us. The lot backed up to a greenbelt, and I could imagine the wonderful landscaping potential it offered. When I called Susan, I could hear in her voice that my excitement was contagious and that she was becoming enthused, too, even without having seen the house yet. I could also tell that she felt more comfortable with my assessment because, this time, things felt right, and I was no longer in such a frantic emotional space. *Now* we were flowing. I told our real-estate agent to make an offer on the house, and the seller accepted our offer the same day.

But as with many purchases of a house, a number of stumbling blocks still began to get in our way—so many, in fact, that to relate them all would fill this book! The owner of the house was not adept at communication and follow-through. Again and again he failed to meet the requirements of the contract, and there were times I thought we might have to back out of the purchase.

It was disappointing to be mired down again when, for a bit, things had begun to flow for us. I spent many hours on the phone with Susan, and together we asked for guidance on what we should do. Should we move on? When each of us asked this question, the answer that came back to both of us was to *be patient.* Be patient—not an easy thing to do, when the issue was so emotional for both of us. Moreover, it was a matter of principle for me. The owner's approach to the negotiations and transactions were just bad business, and I was growing more and more resentful of his behavior.

Finally, my frustration and the lack of forward motion overcame me. In exasperation one night I told Spirit, "I put this in your hands." I was done. If we got the house, I would be happy. If not, I was prepared to continue the search.

And with that, as if by magic, the owner showed a complete change of attitude. He began to communicate with us and to fulfill his obligations to finalize the sale of the house. Just a few weeks after I turned the situation over to Spirit we found ourselves closing at the title company, and on February 22, 2000, I moved into the house. Shortly thereafter, Susan moved to San Antonio. We were exactly where we had dreamed of being—together and in a home where we were happy and could build our lives together.

- - - - - - - - - - - - - - -

This chapter is about *patience*, and I chose this story to illustrate the value of patience because there were so many lessons given to me throughout this process. Through it, I was shown, again and again, the value of being patient. While I felt a great deal of pressure to find a house, and had to focus on our future, what was transpiring was also teaching me to pay attention. I was being shown how to be present in the moment, to recognize when things were not flowing, to take that lack of flow as a sign and ask for guidance.

I was being taught that my old way of coping with resistance, which had been to push against it and overcome it, no matter what it took, was not always the best way. Through this process I had come to understand that resistance could well be Spirit sending me messages that the universe had a better outcome for me than the one I envisioned. The lack of flow, in many ways, originated with me, because I was putting pressure on myself and remaining attached to the outcome.

And another lesson I learned was that the universe sometimes conceives of more abundance for me than I imagine for myself. I had thought the best thing for us was to have a house much like those I had owned before. I had never thought that something new, something different from what I envisioned, might bring us so much joy. I had almost missed out on this wonderful gift because I had been trying to control everything.

Looking back, I realized that, through much of the process, I had not been present, relaxed, and open to new opportunities. Instead of focusing on working with God, I had become focused on all of the wrong things. Instead of slowing down to allow opportunities to unfold, I had tried to rush the entire process.

Above all, the lesson I was taught was the value of patience. Patience brings so many gifts to those who are willing to embrace it. Patience opens the way for Spirit to guide my life. Through patience, my only task is to pay attention and let things unfold in an unforced way. In practicing patience and accessing Spirit, I begin to embrace and see the sacred in life.

Every time my wife and I go walking in the neighborhood, we walk by "the other house," and I am reminded again of the gifts I received through patience. My wife laughs at me as we pass the other house—she knows I cringe inside when I see it, reminded again that I nearly bought the wrong house for us. It is in such moments, and with a sense of humor, that I learn to be patient with myself.

- - - - - - - - - - - - - - -

Many times during the day I feel that my emotional, intellectual, and physical body are ahead of my spiritual body. What I mean is that I notice my focus is on reacting, analyzing, or rushing around instead of being focused on the moment. When I am scattered and unfocused, I find myself impatient. Patience has more to do with my spiritual body, where peace and my inner guidance reside. What can I do to remain patient during my day?

My Thoughts—

"Spirit is the real and eternal: matter is the unreal and temporal."

—Mary Baker Eddy

David D. Dameron

I know there are two main areas on which I can work to be more patient: control and expectations. When I try to control what I want to happen, I am sometimes disappointed when things do not work out. When acting from a place of control, I can also miss opportunities that I mistake for setbacks. Then, there are times when I expect something to happen, and when it does not, I become impatient. That impatience keeps me from being present in the moment. The great lesson I receive again and again is that *Spirit* is in control. My task is to remain present and let events unfold. How can I best do this?

My Thoughts—

"A watched pot never boils."

—Proverb

I received a call from a potential client today, and she told me she does not know whether she will be able to use my services this year. This person is under much stress, and she cannot seem to make a decision that will, in reality, help her reduce her stress by utilizing my services. She is frustrated, and I am frustrated for her. It is in these moments that I call upon my patience. I realize that if I am meant to help this woman, I will be given a way to do that, without forcing the situation or walking away. My way of interacting with this woman—calmly and confidently—shows me that I am making progress with my patience. Can you think of examples of moments in which you are practicing patience well? What signs tell you that you are practicing patience?

My Thoughts—

"Patience is a virtue."

—Proverb

David D. Dameron

Here is a technique I use to work on being patient. For this technique to work, you must believe there is a Higher Power guiding your life. The technique is to approach every person and every event, each day, as a gift sent to directly you and your life toward some successful conclusion or realization. Through guidance from our Higher Power we are being invited to pay attention, to realize the gift each person or event brings. I believe that everything we desire is meant to happen for us. Sometimes when one door appears to close, another one opens. God is patience.

My Thoughts—

"The bud may have a
bitter taste, but sweet
will be the flower."

—William Cowper

Today I drove to several stained-glass shops to arrange to have a stained-glass window constructed for my office. I could not find the first shop I looked for. The second shop was not open. I began to feel impatient, since I had taken the day off to concentrate on this project and was making no progress. I finally gave up and decided to do another errand. As I was driving to another store, I drove by a stained-glass business that was not on my list. My little voice said to go in, so I stopped and went in and immediately fell in love with the store and the artwork they offered. They ended up making an exquisite stained-glass window for me. This process was an example of the rewards of being patient and paying attention. Whatever we desire will eventually be attracted to us! Have you ever had a similar situation happen to you?

My Thoughts—

"Everything comes to
him who waits."

—Proverb

I have been indirectly involved in the disposition of my parents' estate, and the progress has been slow. Since I am not the estate's executor, I often have to make room for the other parties involved and their differing styles of doing business. At times I have found myself becoming impatient, but my guidance has remained clear: non-action. Sometimes taking no action is the best thing to do in a situation. I made it a point to remove my emotions from this situation, and things began unfolding better. I am learning to be flexible and tolerant of other people's methodologies.

My Thoughts—

"Patience and passage of time do more than strength and fury."

—Jean de la Fontaine

My swimming pool sometimes gets extremely dirty, especially after a thunderstorm. When I go out to clean it, I find myself looking at the debris in it and feeling impatient about how long cleaning it will take. I've found the job goes more quickly if I focus on one section at a time, rather than focusing on the whole pool and the entire task. I am wondering how I can use this awareness in other areas of my life.

My Thoughts—

"First things first."

—Proverb

David D. Dameron

I have spent the greater part of this year writing and producing my first book. I let almost all of my clients go at the beginning of this year so I could concentrate on this project. Now that the book is complete, I am trying to build my business again, and at times my progress seems slow. This is a great opportunity to let Spirit do my marketing. With Spirit marketing, my job is to pay attention and recognize opportunities. Instead of calling prospective clients and trying to control the growth, I have been patient, letting my business grow with Spirit in control. This has been hard for me, since I am more used to taking the traditional method—"get out and knock on the doors." But the unexpected opportunities that present themselves affirm that I am rewarded by my patience.

My Thoughts—

"Rome was not built in
a day."

—Proverb

I affirm each day that Spirit is guiding my life. I need do only two things: first, envision in my mind's eye what I desire; and second, affirm in each moment that I will be led to know what I need to do to fulfill that vision. In letting Spirit guide me, I remain aware that life is about "ebbs and flows." Knowing when to act and when to wait requires patience. I will not force change. The doors will open to show me the way. This is my new commitment to bring forth my divinity.

My Thoughts—

"Wait and see."

—Herbert Henry Asquith

David D. Dameron

In my meditation today I asked for guidance about the present condition of my business and my finances because I want to build up my business. What is hilarious is that my income this month was only $187.50. I have not made that kind of money since I was in high school and working for my father. I actually laugh at myself about how calm I am about my finances. I just feel things are going to pick up again soon. How about tomorrow, Spirit?

My Thoughts—

"We must learn to walk
before we can run."

—Proverb

I took my son to Austin today because he had a meeting he needed to attend. His meeting started at 3:00 p.m. and was to last about an hour. So I did some sightseeing in Austin and came back to pick him up at 4:00, but as it turned out, he did not finish his meeting until 5:30. I sat in the car, feeling impatient and wanting to get back to San Antonio. Suddenly I had a feeling that there was a good reason for the delay. I turned on the radio and found out that one of the towns we travel through going back to San Antonio had been struck by a tornado. If we had left on time, we would have passed through the town at the exact time the tornado hit. I remind all of you how important it is to realize that allowing events to unfold naturally can sometimes save your life.

My Thoughts—

"In the now is all time, and to understand the now is to be free of time."

—J. Krishnamurti

David D. Dameron

The doors to my business picking up went flying open today. The telephone rang all day with people wanting to engage my services. I heard from people I had not talked to in over a year. By the end of the day, I was both grateful and worn out. What an emotional rollercoaster I have been on! I keep reminding myself to be patient and look at life with my spiritual eyes. My spiritual eyes see Spirit at work all of the time for me—even when it seems to me the telephone is not ringing. In Spirit's realm, it is only a matter of time before events unfold. To approach my life with this knowledge is to see the sacred in life. I am in such awe of life.

My Thoughts—

"Thus there are these two streams, one from the past and one from the future, which come together in the Soul—will anyone who observes himself deny that?"

—Rudolph Steiner

CHAPTER ELEVEN:

PRAYER

"Prayer may be the single most powerful force in creation. Individually, we are given the silent language that allows us to participate in the outcome of events and the challenges of our lives. Together, mass prayer is our opportunity to share in the outcome of our world."

—Gregg Braden, *The Isaiah Effect*

One of my favorite authors and workshop trainers is Gregg Braden, who has written four books that I recommend highly. In his best-selling book, entitled *The Isaiah Effect*,* Gregg recounts of a lesson he learned from David, a Native-American medicine man.

The book tells the story of a hike Gregg took with David through the mountains in northern New Mexico. The area where they hiked had been in the grip of a severe drought, and the needs of the land were evident all around them as they hiked. They were making their way to a sacred spot where David had said he would show Gregg how Native Americans create rain, a process he described as "to pray rain."

David took Gregg to a special spot in the mountains, where there was a circle of stones on the ground. He explained that the stone circle served as a medicine wheel and its purpose was to help one focus as one walked the circle. He added, "We will invite the rain today," and David removed his shoes and began walking the circle, digging his toes into the soil as he walked.

When he finished walking the circle, David put his shoes on, and he and Gregg walked back down the mountain. Along the way, he pointed out to Gregg that he was "praying rain, and not praying *for* rain," because, David said, praying *for* rain would not have the effect he wanted—it would not bring rain.

That afternoon, though weather reports had stated there was no end to the drought in sight, Gregg watched as clouds began to gather. The smell of rain was in the air, and soon the rain began, nourishing the New Mexico desert that had been in a drought for quite some time.

Gregg asked David how he had been able to bring the rain and why praying for it directly was not advisable. David said his approach was not to ask for rain through prayer; rather, the success of his attempt to bring rain hinged on connection and emotion. The key to his prayer, he said, was *feeling* what it would be like if it rained. When David was walking the circle, he felt his toes digging into wet soil. He felt his body getting wet from the rainfall.

His prayer had become a prayer of gratitude to the invisible forces that make all things happen, for rain that had already come. David said that the rain had always been present, ready to be invited. His prayer was merely a matter of choosing the creation he wanted to experience.

---

* Author's Note: *The Isaiah Effect* is published by Three Rivers Press, New York, New York. Member of the Crown Publishing Group.

- - - - - - - - - - - - - - -

This chapter is about *prayer*. When I read Gregg Braden's telling of the above story, I was reminded of the role of the "Faithkeeper" in Native-American tradition. The Faithkeeper is the tribe member whose role is to remain at peace, centered in the spiritual vision for the tribe, and to maintain this vigilance no matter what else transpires.

In other words, the Faithkeeper envisions perfection for the tribe, with all its needs and desires provided. The approaches of the Faithkeeper and David, the medicine man, are very similar.

In the Western tradition, we have been taught for centuries that prayer is about asking for help, or asking for a situation to be healed. But another approach to prayer, and, I believe, a more effective one, is to use prayer as a bridge for bringing to us what has already been provided. Our only duty is to claim, through prayer, what we want in our conscious mind.

To *claim* it. To see and feel what we desire and to act as if what we desire has already been given—which, in reality, it has. The challenge for mankind is to break through the veil that separates our desires from what we perceive as our reality. Most people raised in the Western tradition pray as though there were a force outside of themselves, and they pray to that force, asking for intervention against war, violence, and disease, or asking that force to manifest a change in their life or in their world.

The reality is that war, violence, and disease are choices. Poverty is a choice. And once you accept that these things are *choices,* it becomes clear that there are other alternatives available from which to choose.

Imagine the shift on this planet and in your own life—imagine what would be possible—if, instead of being based on what you *don't* have, your prayers were centered in what you already *do* have: the rain that is waiting for an invitation, the world peace that is already with us. Instead of being based on supplication, your prayers would be praises of gratitude for desires already fulfilled.

How about a prayer seeing prosperity, perfect health, and social justice for all? How about a prayer for peace—peace that exists throughout the world, and a vision of all people sustaining it by acting in peace? Imagine that the world you would pray for already exists, and see the world as a living reflection of your prayer.

One of the keys to this approach to prayer is to remain totally present and focused in the moment. So to pray for peace means, first, finding peace within yourself, and knowing, beyond a shadow of a doubt, that peace is already available to you, to all of us. When you find peace within yourself—when you tap the power of manifestation through prayer—then you will see the sacred in life!

When we infuse our prayers with feeling, we bring into manifestation whatever we are envisioning. What you desire, what you long for in your life and in your world, is available to you right now—it always has been and always will be. This is our divine inheritance, an inheritance I write about often, and that is our greatest gift. It only requires that you recognize the gift and access it, and that choice is yours to make!

David D. Dameron

Each day my prayers shall be about perfection and not imperfection; not my own perfection, but that of my divinity. I pray to bring my divinity forth in its perfection, for my own sake and for the sake of others as well. Each and every one of my thoughts, words, and actions is a reflection of who I am. Each reflects whether I am living my life from my divinity or my ego. I will strive to remember to declare who I am, what I am, and who I choose to be in thought, words, and action. If I am willing to accept myself as a divine being, then my prayers should be nothing less than perfection.

My Thoughts—

"The wings of prayer
carry high and far."

—Anonymous

Our future is filled with many possibilities, but none of those possibilities has yet occurred. Standing in the present moment, our possible futures exist merely as reflections of the choices we are making in the present. Our prayers should not be for possible futures, but for preferred outcomes of benefit to ourselves and to others. Peace, prosperity and mutual respect are possible outcomes for everyone on this planet if we can hold that vision in our consciousness. Instead of praying for peace to come about, it is time for us to *see* peace, inside and outside of ourselves. The power of prayer is that it is a proactive way to establish what we wish our desires and intentions to be.

My Thoughts—

"Prayer is the spirit
speaking truth to Truth."

—Philip James Bailey

David D. Dameron

I write often about the power of our thoughts, feelings, and actions. Everything that occurs in our external world is a reflection of what is occurring inside each of us. Prayer is a tool we can use to *focus* our thoughts and feelings. Again, when you pray, see and feel perfection. Know that your prayer is like throwing a rock into a pond, the ripples extending throughout the universe and, eventually, returning to you.

My Thoughts—

"It is not well for man to pray cream, and live skim milk."

—Henry Ward Beecher

Prayer and gratitude are intimately connected. As I have said, by the nature of our divine inheritance, everything we need has already been created for us. Our task is to claim it in our consciousness. Therefore, prayers are most effective when, rather than asking that something manifest, they instead express gratitude for that which has *already been given*. It follows that what manifests is what we have chosen. We can choose, for example, to envision peace for this planet. If peace already exists, then why do we continue to choose war? Remember that we are evolving our consciousness and our awareness. Our prayers should envision a world of divine beings making choices that do not bring harm to anyone. The power of prayer is an awesome force.

My Thoughts—

"When thou prayest, rather let thy heart be without words than thy words without heart."

—John Bunyan

David D. Dameron

Each day I surround the people and things in my life with love and a prayer of protection. I see only perfection. I envision my house being protected. I circle my children in loving thoughts, seeing them as being complete and safe. I circle my wife and her school in loving thoughts, knowing that her children, teachers, and parents are safe and perfect. I surround my daily affairs and people I work with during the day with loving thoughts. With every workshop I teach, I envision the room being a safe environment where people are affected in a positive way by what I teach. And finally, I surround myself in a prayer for my own divinity, giving thanks that I am alive and fulfilling my purpose.

My Thoughts—

"Prayer ... the very highest energy of which the mind is capable."

—Samuel Taylor Coleridge

Because my prayers engage the power of my subconscious, I am not surprised that my prayers sometimes become part of my dreams. Last night I was given three signs in my dreams. One was an ape (like King Kong), which I see as symbolic of my need to claim my power and my divinity. The second image was of fish hooks caught in my hand—I saw this as a sign of good fortune. And third, I was walking along a path that had signs with an S on them, like the Superman symbol. The S was representative of my divinity coming forth, or my "super man." What do your dreams tell you about your thoughts, and your prayers?

My Thoughts—

"Prayer should be the key of the day and the lock at night."

—ThomasFule

217

David D. Dameron

Today I taught the fifth-graders at my wife's school some techniques to help them be better organized. During the session, I asked them to silently wish for something they really would like to have in their lives. Since most of the children at my wife's school come from disadvantaged homes, I was amazed at how hard it was for them to visualize something they could wish for. Then I realized that their world is not about possibility. In my prayer for these children today, I saw each child as a divine being—perfect and aware that he or she is abundant and fulfilled. At some point in their lives these children, like all of us, will have to claim their divinity in order to truly realize their desires.

My Thoughts—

"Those who always pray are necessary to those who never pray."

—Victor Hugo

I have been part of several healing groups for years. As a participant, on a weekly and monthly basis, I am given a list of individuals who are facing a personal challenge. These people have requested prayers. My duty is to envision a positive outcome for these individuals in my prayers. I do not need to know them personally nor do I need to be near them geographically for my prayers to have an effect; the power of prayer knows no boundaries. Prayer connects all of us, wherever we live and whomever we know.

My Thoughts—

"Prayer does not change
God, but changes him
who prays."

—Søren Kierkegaard

David D. Dameron

In 1968, I had the wonderful opportunity of traveling to Europe with some of my high school friends and my foreign language teacher. My fondest memories are of visiting many of the ancient churches in Europe. When I walked into these cathedrals, I could feel the energy still present from the thousands of people who had prayed there down through the centuries. I remember sitting down on a bench in one of the churches and just sinking into the silence. Like a blanket, the warmth of the many prayers that had been offered there settled around me. I realized years later that prayer is a form of energy. It is palpable. Prayer is an awesome force.

My Thoughts—

"Prayers travel more strongly when said in unison."

—Petronius

To be effective, prayer must be focused in the present. If our thoughts are scattered, then our prayers, too, will be scattered and ineffective. Prayer is a tool for personal growth that we can use to focus our thoughts and our hearts on positive outcomes for ourselves and for others. When I see peace marches and vigils being conducted by large groups of people, I am reminded that focused prayer is more powerful than any weapon mankind might possess. The Bible states that "Where two or more are gathered, I will be there." Each time we pray, know that the Divine is part of the process and is with us. Prayers help us see the sacred in life, and, with them, we can change the world.

My Thoughts—

"Prayer is dangerous business. Results do come."

—G. Christie Swain

CHAPTER TWELVE:

SURRENDER

"Surrender is not just a religious concept; it's a power tool for listening to the voice of your spirit and following its directions ... to find the real meaning and the power of surrender, practice releasing and letting go—just loving. This is not giving up. Surrender is a process of stilling and emptying the mind."

—Sara Paddison, *The Hidden Power of the Heart*

In 1985, I resigned my position as sales manager for a retail company in San Antonio. Over the previous months, I had realized that something was missing in my life, and I decided part of what was missing was that I desperately wanted to start my own business.

On a deeper level, though, I was feeling disconnected from my spirit. As a result of losing touch with my sprit, I was feeling disconnected from all aspects of my personal and professional life.

What transpired once I decided to honor my spirit and resign my position as a sales manager was one of the most mysterious series of events that have ever happened to me. The events that followed showed me that life can be a rollercoaster, with many ups and downs.

A gentleman reappeared in my life at this time who had been an employee of mine when I owned a small bookstore in San Antonio in the early 1980s. His name was Jonathan, and he called me to say he was visiting San Antonio again, having traveled to Texas from his home in Scotland.

Jonathan was a former priest and he taught a spiritual philosophy called *A Course in Miracles* and counseled drug addicts in Scotland. He had been very successful in helping individuals to break their addictions and get their lives back on track. He said he had come to San Antonio to visit some friends, and said he'd like to come by and see me again one evening, just to say hello. I was glad to hear from him again; I had always found him to be a trustworthy and interesting young man with whom I always felt safe.

Jonathan came by my house around 8:00 one evening, and after some casual conversation he asked me how I was REALLY doing. I broke down and began crying. I told Jonathan everything that was wrong with my life both professionally and personally.

He listened intently and began performing his "counseling magic" on me. By 2:00 a.m. Jonathan had transformed me. He had helped me to feel God's presence in my life again, and had re-instilled in me the knowledge that I had the power to manifest anything I desired in my life.

Jonathan left that evening after letting me know that he was part of an inner circle of wealthy individuals in England and Scotland, and that these individuals were looking for projects in which to invest. He said that if I ever came up with a business idea to let him know.

In my renewed, heightened state of feeling divinely connected, Jonathan's offer was like giving a kid a blank check in a toy store. I had been forming an idea for a company and I felt very enthused about it, and after Jonathan left I went to work on a business plan.

When I'd finished, I sent him the plan, saying I was trying to raise one hundred and fifty thousand dollars in capital. I was really excited; I felt my life had taken a turn for the better, and this company would put me back on track.

I couldn't wait to get Jonathan's response and I finally called him in Scotland. He said he had received my letter and the business plan, and he thought the plan outlined a good idea. He said he would show it immediately to the group of investors.

I was on cloud nine; everything seemed to be falling into place. In the autumn of 1986, Jonathan called to tell me that the investors liked my idea. He suggested that I get a passport and be prepared to fly to England to meet with them.

He also informed me that he was going through a nasty divorce and that his attention would be split between his work, his divorce, and working on my deal. He assured me, however, that my project would be a high priority.

By January of 1987, I had called Scotland several times to speak with Jonathan. My telephone bill looked like the national debt. My telephone bill wasn't the only financial challenge; I was so excited that I had begun using some of my personal savings to start setting up some aspects of my company. Each time I spoke with Jonathan I updated him on the steps I was taking, and each time he assured me everything was okay.

But by February I was becoming concerned. My intuition was screaming at me that something was not right. I called Jonathan, expressing my concerns, and he promised to call me in two weeks with the final details of our business arrangement and the financing.

Two weeks passed and I had heard nothing. I waited one more week, and then I decided I had to call Jonathan. I dialed the number; it was the same number I had dialed several times over the past few months and at which I'd always reached him. But this time there was no ringing of the telephone. There was nothing!

I called the international operator and told her I was calling a city in Scotland and that I was not hearing a ring on the other end. She asked me for the number, and I gave it to her. After dialing it herself, she informed me that not only was the number I gave her a non-working number—it was not even the prefix for Scotland!

I was dumbfounded. I explained to the operator that I had several hundreds of dollars in long distance telephone bills sitting in front of me indicating that the city I was calling was in Scotland.

The operator reaffirmed that there must have been a mistake on the telephone bill. I promptly hung up on that operator and called another international operator, only to be told the same thing.

It was beginning to sink in that something was desperately wrong with all of this, but I held onto hope. I did not want to believe that I was being stopped—for some reason—from trying to fund this company.

To this day I have never heard from Jonathan. Through a mutual friend, I did learn that Jonathan's divorce had taken an emotional toll on him, causing him to lose his home and to suffer financially.

And in time I began to see that I had not really known how to put an effective business plan together; nor did I have some of the skills, at that time, to run a company such as the one I had designed in the plan.

So, without much choice, I began to let go of the idea, in spite of all my hopes. I instead pursued a position as a freelance consultant for a company; that job eventually led me to starting my own training and consulting business, a business much better suited to my skills and business expertise.

- - - - - - - - - - - - - -

This chapter is about *surrender*. I had some difficulty in writing about this event because it took me years to even begin to understand what happened with Jonathan.

What I eventually came to understand is that it is very hard to accept that we cannot always be in control. We sometimes find it comforting to think that, because we have the power of choice and we have the power to conceive new ideas, we can control all the events in our life.

We set goals and make plans, and we become obsessed with the need for those goals to manifest in our lives. We let ourselves believe that we can make anything happen.

Inevitably, life sends each of us challenges that completely alter our belief in our ability to control every detail of our lives. The failure of my venture with Jonathan to manifest taught me that, at some point, I had let go of everything I desired and expected, and let events unfold in their own unique way.

I see an intimate connection between faith and surrender. It took faith to surrender my emotions and my insecurities in this situation. Ultimately, I had to draw upon my faith that the Divine had a hand in this affair and was looking out for my best interests, no matter how things seemed. That faith gave me strength to surrender my emotions and my desires to something greater than myself.

At some point in our lives, no matter what is happening to us, we must acknowledge that the Divine is with us, as always, and surrender to forces beyond our control, trusting in the Divine to support us. When we have done everything we can do to participate in the emergence of something we desire, our final task is to turn that desire over to God and say, "Thy will be done."

Surrender does not mean giving up your vision of what you desire. Rather, it means trusting TOTALLY in what transpires. I have found that I need to monitor my expectations when working towards bringing a desire to fruition. I have also discovered that often, in the course of moving toward what I desire, I will realize that I am not in control of the outcome.

All I can do is set my intention in my consciousness and believe and act as if it is going to manifest according to my vision. And accept that, ultimately, things will turn out exactly the way they are supposed to.

So in the final analysis, surrender is not about GIVING UP. It is about LETTING GO. It is an act that brings forth our divinity and brings us into alignment with our Higher Self.

- - - - - - - - - - - - - -

When I worry about something, I am denying my power and the ability to work from my spirit. Instead of seeing a situation as a problem, I should envision it as being perfect, and let go of the outcome. This is the attitude of surrender. Surrender is about living my life in perfection, and in order for me to see perfection, I must accept that perfection inside myself, for I am a divine being.

My Thoughts—

"He who knows others is wise; he who knows himself is enlightened."

—Lao-Tzu

David D. Dameron

Today my affirmation is, "I accept the Holy Vision." God is everywhere, all-knowing, and all-powerful. I am an aspect of the Divine and I am part of the Holy Vision; that means I am part of perfection and all-sufficiency. I surrender any thoughts to the contrary. No matter what is occurring in my life, I trust totally in the holy presence, and my life, my actions, and my thoughts and words are a reflection of my divinity.

My Thoughts—

"Everything   flows, nothing stays still."

—Heraclitus

I realized today that, since the Divine is everywhere, there is not a single event occurring in my life that I am not experiencing in Spirit. Everything is God. Everything in my life is a mirror of my choices, or the choices of someone else. My task is to see events with my spiritual eyes and know that everything in the universe is an expression of a thought, an idea, or an action. I wish I were more vigilant and aware of this truth when I am facing my challenges. I sometimes forget that challenges are gifts the Divine has sent me. My present focus should be surrendering to the moment and remembering that the Divine is part of ALL events in my life.

My Thoughts—

"To see a world in a grain
of sand and a heaven in a
wild flower, hold infinity
in the palm of your hand
and eternity in an hour."

—William Blake

The only thing I give up when I surrender is my sense of separation from Spirit. Either I believe I am a divine being and all is in perfect order, and act from that place, or I do not. Thus, surrender takes place within my being without me having to give up anything. I affirm, "I let it go and I let it flow." That is the ultimate step that we all must take at some point in our lives. The ultimate surrender is acceptance—acceptance of our divinity! What keeps me from accepting this truth all of the time?

My Thoughts—

"One in all, All in me—
If only this is realized,
no more worry about
you not being perfect."

—Swan the Third Zen Patriarch

My house is in the middle of remodeling, and I realize the walls the builders are constructing are a mirror of the walls I feel inside myself. The house is in disarray, and I cannot get any work done because my office is under construction. I want the workers to finish and get out of my life. It is in these moments that I am not present and my thoughts are unfocused and scattered. I must learn to surrender my circumstances when I am not in control. When these situations, and the frustration they can cause, put me out of touch with my spirit, surrender is the only way for me to reconnect.

My Thoughts—

"What will be, will be, grumble who may."

—Anne Boleyn

David D. Dameron

I asked in my meditation this morning how I can best assist evolving my life spiritually at this point. The answers that came back to me were *truth and integrity*; that I be honest with myself and true to my beliefs in all activities and actions. That I let go of anything that does not mirror my highest intentions. That I release my desires and needs to the Divine and surrender my problems and concerns.

My Thoughts—

"Running water will run faster if you remove an obstruction here and there. You need not do much more."

—Yogaswami

I can feel that my consulting and training business is about to pick up. I have learned to wait for doors to open before I start knocking. That is a new approach for me, and it is contrary to how I have gone about attracting clients in the past. Now that I am waiting, while focused in the present moment, I find that I pay attention better. Ultimately, the true surrender is to be totally focused on what is occurring in the moment and to do so with love, joy, and enthusiasm. It is nice to know that I am not alone in my daily challenges and activities.

My Thoughts—

"Unless one says good-bye to what one loves, and unless one travels to completely new territories, one can expect merely a long wearing away of oneself and eventual extinction."

—Jean Dubuffet

David D. Dameron

    I am having some difficulty with my publisher over the production of my first book. One of the customer service people I am working with does not understand how my books are to be laid out. The book continues to be produced incorrectly, in spite of a number of telephone calls and repeated explanations. I finally became so exasperated that I just surrendered the situation to Spirit and asked to be shown what to do. A thought came to me to call another lady at the publisher that I'd successfully worked with when I originally submitted my manuscript. As it turned out, she was able to assist me and solve my problem. I am reminded in these situations of an old saying, "Ask, and ye shall receive."

My Thoughts—

"You have to endure
what you can't change."

—Marie De France

I was teaching a class today that I have not taught in months, and I was a little nervous and uncomfortable. As the participants entered the room, I felt myself becoming quite anxious. I took a deep breath and said to myself and my spirit, "Let your words be my words." In this moment of surrender, I found myself delivering one the best workshops I have ever given. I felt myself relax, and I also experienced an incredible connection with my spirit. I am learning so much about surrender.

My Thoughts—

"I think that all human systems require continuous renewal ... of having things the way they have always been, appeals to a supposedly happy past. But we've got to move on."

—John W. Gardiner

David D. Dameron

I was talking to a friend today about the concept of surrender, and his concept of it was that surrender meant giving up. I said that I did not see it that way. I felt surrender was just a way of getting myself out of the way and letting Spirit orchestrate things. When I do surrender, I feel that my attitude and outlook on life are transformed. I need to remember that Spirit is in control. I appreciated my friend helping to clarify what surrender means to me.

My Thoughts—

"The ultimate aim of man is liberation; liberation not only from the bondage of the flesh, but also from the limitation of a finite being."

—Anonymous

I was watching a professional golf tournament on television today. Several golfers were being interviewed, and I found it interesting that each was saying the same thing and repeating it over and over. They were talking about staying focused and in the moment. They said it was important for them not to worry about a previous shot or a future hole. They kept talking about staying "within yourself," centered, and concentrating only on one shot at a time, the shot before them. I was reminded about surrendering to the moment, an approach I write about often. My new mantra is, "There is only the moment, and each moment is perfect."

My Thoughts—

"Liberation and enlightenment do not exist outside of your own self. We need only open our eyes to see that we ourselves are the very essence of liberation and enlightenment."

—Thich Nhat Hanh

David D. Dameron

I realized today that surrender is really about liberation and freedom. It is about breaking free of the material world and not becoming overly attached to what happens in my external world. When I surrender events in my life to Spirit, I am tapping into my inner nature, where the source of my true power resides. In doing so, I am freeing and liberating my spirit. My outer life then becomes a mirror of my inner liberation. When someone asks me how they can change something in their life, I will have them read this passage: "Change the inside, change the outside." When I approach change in this way and surrender, I see the sacred in life!

My Thoughts—

"As rivers flow into the sea and in so doing lose name and form, even so the wise man freed from name and form, attracts the Supreme Being, the Self-luminous, the Infinite."

—*The Upanishads*

CHAPTER THIRTEEN:

REVERENCE

"Ah, you have told me one more thing. You are grateful and gratitude is the recognition of grace. And the recognition of grace testifies that I am the only power and the only life that is operating in your life. Thank you, my love, for your gratitude. Your gratitude is the kiss that has bonded us together into eternal oneness."

—Walter Starcke, *Homesick for Heaven*

I received a call today that shook me to the very core of my being. In an instant, my world crumbled as if I had been in the middle of an earthquake. The telephone call concerned my son, who had called his mom to inform her that there had been an accident and that he was okay. My son had just left to attend a geological field camp through the university he attends.

Early this morning I had driven him from San Antonio to Austin. He had with him a backpack and a duffle bag full of clothes, enough for a six-week adventure in Colorado, where he would conduct various geological experiments.

We had encountered some rain going to Austin, but even so, we arrived early, partly due to my inclination to arrive early for appointments or destinations. Though the parking lot had few people when we first arrived, within a few minutes four vans from the university geology department pulled into the parking lot. The vans would carry several professors and teaching assistants, who would be directing the field camp this summer, and the students, like my son, who were attending.

I left my son standing on the sidewalk, his baggage beside him as he waited for the other twenty or so students to arrive. I had to hurry back home for an appointment I had that morning. I remember saying good-bye to my son, and then I drove back to San Antonio.

My son later told me that the vans with the students left the campus that morning around 7:00 a.m. and began their journey through West Texas; their route would take them through New Mexico to Colorado. Somewhere in West Texas the group encountered a rainstorm.

The van my son was in was third in the line of four vans traveling down the interstate. Suddenly, my son said they saw, through the rain, the van that had been traveling directly in front them. The scene was horrific—the van had flipped over several times, and several of the passengers had been thrown from the vehicle. A geology professor and a student in the van had been killed, and the other passengers were critically injured and were taken to the hospital.

When I received the call from my son's mother, my first concern was the health of my son; as soon as I was certain he was all right, my heart went out to the families of the injured and killed.

I realized, when I got off the telephone with my son's mother, that I was somewhat in shock. The more I thought about the tragedy as the evening went on, the more upset I became. I cried all night. I could not sleep. My mind was racing with the many issues this event had raised for me.

- - - - - - - - - - - - - -

As a parent, I have the same wish I think most every parent has: that my children will outlive me and live happy and fulfilling lives. Today's events reminded me painfully how fragile life is. You never know when, through unexpected circumstances, someone you love will be taken away.

But the events also brought up several questions I knew I had to face and answer. My mind went back to the early part of this year, when my son was given a choice: to seek an internship with a company in the area of his specialty as a summer job, or to attend field camp.

He had been leaning toward the internship, but I steered him away from it for many reasons. I thought the field camp would be easier to arrange than finding an internship would be.

That night, as I couldn't sleep and looked back at the events of the day, I found myself wondering whether I had urged him toward camp to accommodate my own needs rather than his. Had my son been led to do the internship? In urging him to go to the camp, had I interfered with his own relationship with Spirit? He did eventually choose to do the field camp by his own choice, but I felt compelled to look at my involvement in this situation. I felt a need to understand the circumstances that led up to today's tragedy, and to understand the forces at work that brought my son close to danger, but spared him.

Other questions came into play. What made my son pick the van that he traveled in? Was getting there early that morning a contributing factor to his choice of vans, or could it be my desire to always be early had worked against me this morning?

My wife gently reminded me that I was being too hard on myself as I processed this tragedy. She reminded me that I could play "what if"'s all day, but the bottom line was that he was not injured, and we should be thankful for that.

I realized today that, in spite of all of my spiritual and personal growth work, I was clearly not equipped to handle the potential loss of my son. Could I have forgiven myself if something had happened to him? Could the pressure I put on him to choose this summer trip possibly have caused his death, or come close to doing so?

Was I listening to my guidance in guiding my son in his decision making? Why was my son spared, and what lessons did this event hold for all of us? After I had dissected the day's events a hundred times in my mind, the lesson I was to learn finally came to me.

I learned that, ultimately, I am not in control what happens in other people's lives or in my own. As much as I may try to protect my children and others I care about from harm, each of our lives carries a lesson and a purpose, and when our time comes, it just comes.

I was also reminded that I need to pay attention to each moment and ask on a moment-by-moment basis what choice I should make. And then I need to let go of that choice and put it in the hands of Spirit. This is the lesson of surrender at work again in my life.

Life is so very sacred. Each moment is precious. I have such reverence for life, even though this event with my son was quite unnerving and personally painful in terms of what I had to face about myself.

But I cannot unravel the past and do anything about the choices I have made. I can only focus on being in this present moment, and choose to learn from this tragedy or any future challenge that I might face.

I thank God that my son was spared, and I have grown in awareness from this event for which I am also thankful. My reverence for life was deepened, and I became even more aware that my daily task is to be willing to turn my life over to Spirit in each moment. In doing so, I strengthen my ability to see the sacred in life—whatever may come.

- - - - - - - - - - - - - - -

David D. Dameron

I worked with a client today and as I was dialoguing with her, I realized that my insights were helping her through a difficult crisis. I am reminded in these moments that my life does have a purpose, and that purpose is helping others find more productive ways to lead their lives. But there is a deeper insight I had today, and that was that I have a deep reverence I have for life. We are here in this lifetime to help one another. I was helping my client, but she was also helping me by allowing my gift—my ability to advise people—to emerge. What other situations remind me that I hold life in reverence?

My Thoughts—

"Always and in everything let there be reverence."

—Confucius

My wife and I have discussed many times that how we chose to live our lives seems to have a strong impact on others. A couple who are close friends of ours came to stay with us, and they remarked how comfortable and inviting our home was. They also seemed to be affected by how affectionate and playful my wife and I are together. When it came time to say good-bye, our friends remarked that being with us had made them realize there were areas of their own relationship they wanted to work to improve. What this situation taught Susan and me is that, just by living our lives thoughtfully and sincerely, we can help others live their lives in love, kindness, and playfulness as well.

My Thoughts—

"A new heart also will I give you, and a new spirit will I put within you."

—Ezekiel 36:26

David D. Dameron

Whenever I am feeling sluggish or uninspired, my guidance is very clear on how to address the problem—get out into nature. So I go to the park and walk for a while through the trees, and it is in these moments that my reverence for life returns. Nature always seems to reinvigorate me and put me in strong connection with my spirit. I have realized that each time I reconnect with my spirit, I am beginning a new direction in that very moment of reconnection. In what other ways can I connect with my spirit and stay focused in the moment?

My Thoughts—

"If God has spoken, why is the universe not convinced?"

—Percy Bysshe Shelly

I met with a colleague today. She is considering whether to teach a section of an upcoming workshop that I am setting up. She said she went for a walk last week and asked Spirit to send her the person she should work with next. I happened to call her that same morning after her walk and ask her to be part of my workshop. After our meeting, she agreed to teach with me. What a wonderful example of how life operates and meets our needs. Things just seem to work out in a perfect way if we put our intention out sincerely and thoughtfully.

My Thoughts—

"Into thy hands I commend my Spirit."

—John 6:63

David D. Dameron

I am struggling today; some days, despite my work to stay in the present and stay in touch with Spirit, the rhythm of the day is not good. A clear sign that the rhythm is not good is that my interactions with people don't go as well as I'd like. On these days, some people do not return phone calls or they seem short-tempered and impatient. What I have realized is that there are going to be days when the rhythm is just off. I can either go with the flow and take what the day brings, or resist it and make the situation worse. I realized today that enjoying life is learning to follow the flow of life. As much as I would like every day to be perfect, the reality is that this is an unreasonable expectation to put on myself and the universe. Every moment is a gift, a lesson—how can I go with the flow and remain open to the lessons Spirit is sending me?

My Thoughts—

"We treat God with irreverence by banishing him from our thoughts, not by referring to his will on slight occasions."

—John Ruskin

I keep running into this huge, yellow spider in my yard. It makes these wonderful, geometric webs. Today it had moved to a gate entrance to our potting area. My inner voice kept nudging me to look at the location of the spider web. I looked up the meaning of a spider in a Native-American book on the symbolism of animals and insects and found that, in that culture, the spider is a symbol for the infinite possibilities of creation. Then the message became clear: *do not get caught in the illusion of the physical world.* I choose to see beyond the physical world, and remember that polarity can be changed at any time. Remember that you can choose to create, create, create to avoid entangling situations. This encounter with the spider affirms, for me, that life is talking to us all of the time. Life is so sacred and wonderful.

My Thoughts—

"Nature is a revelation
of God; art a revelation
of Man."

—Henry Wadsworth Longfellow

David D. Dameron

If we pay attention, life teaches us in each moment. There are no ordinary moments. Today I was working to proof a magazine article I had written. I'd looked at the article many times, but it had been weeks since I had picked it up. In rereading it today, I saw mistakes I had not seen before. I realized that in relaxing and switching my attention to other projects, I was able to come back to this magazine article and see it as if for the first time. In order to see the perfections and imperfections of life, it is good to approach life in a variety of ways. In what other situations could I keep things fresh by approaching life in a new way?

My Thoughts—

"Let knowledge grow from more to more, But more of reverence in his dwell; That Mind and Soul, according well, May make one music as before."

—Alfred Lord Tennyson

When we are experiencing problems and challenges in our lives, it may feel like God has gone on a vacation and left us alone. The truth is that God works for our good 24\7. The disconnect is with us, not God. We sometimes unplug ourselves from our Spirit because we mistakenly think that challenge and Spirit are separate. The fact is that challenges are our gifts. When you find yourself overwhelmed by the challenges you face, look to the Divine within to straighten out every crooked place. Each moment is a sacred event in creation, despite the form in which it may appear. What situations have you experienced recently in your life that have caused you to disconnect from your Spirit? How might you see those challenges as affirming?

My Thoughts—

"Dear Lord and Father of Mankind, Forgive our foolish ways! Reclothe us in our rightful mind, In purer lives thy service find, In deeper reverence, praise."

—John Greenleaf Whittier

David D. Dameron

Our consciousness is our prayer. If you live your life based on your realization and belief that you are a divine being, then how you live your life affects everyone on this planet. It's a chain of positive change—if you help someone, and your effort results in that person helping someone else, the positive force grows exponentially. At some point everyone on the planet could possibly be positively affected! So I say to each of you: may every wish that you wish for another be a wish that you wish for yourself. For in fact it is. May everything you do be done as if the spirit of God is doing it, for in fact it is. Revere life in each moment.

My Thoughts—

"What do you suppose
will satisfy the soul,
except to walk free and
own no superior?"

—Walt Whitman

I affirm in each moment that the wisdom of God is present for me *now*. The love of God is speaking to me in this moment. I listen to love, and I receive its message. In each moment, I find something to love in everything, for everything is an aspect or expression of the Divine. I am grateful to be alive!

My Thoughts—

"Life is the soul's nursery—its training place for the destinies of eternity."

—William Makepeace Thackeray

David D. Dameron

I believe in the adage, "Until I believe it, I will not see it." Until I believe I am an aspect of the Divine, I will not see myself as part of the Divine. Therefore, I live life as I would like it to be. I think of and imagine life as I would like it to be. I feel life as I would like it to be. I realize that I do not need my physical eyes to see the sacredness of life. My real eyes reside inside my spirit and my consciousness. When I see life from this place of reverence for life, I will then see the sacred in life and, most importantly, I will see the Divine in me.

My Thoughts—

"The windows of my
soul I throw wide open
to the sun."

—John Greenleaf Whittier

I am often asked to explain why, if we are all divine beings on this planet, there is so much violence, crime, and war. My response is: Do not ever lose hope. Life is such a wonderful unfolding. If the world is going to change for the better, each of us must make the personal choice to live our life at the very highest level, by claiming our divinity. I have such reverence for life, and I know one day we will see peace on this planet. I believe peace and prosperity are here now. These are my beliefs. What are yours?

My Thoughts—

"Life is sweet."

—Proverb

AUTHOR'S NOTE

Since I published my first book, *Remembering Our Spirit*, I've been blessed that many of you have shared stories of your adventures and meaningful coincidences with me. Some of those stories are included in this volume. I invite any of you who have inspirational stories to share to send them to me for possible inclusion in future volumes in the *Practical Spirituality Series*. I welcome your responses, whether you are willing to have your story or comments published or not; but if you are willing to have them included in future books, please indicate that. Your name will be kept private.

David D. Dameron
P.O. Box 5911
San Antonio, Texas 78201
www.daviddameron.com

About the Author

David D. Dameron has over thirty years of experience as a teacher, author, trainer, and consultant, helping individuals improve the quality of their lives. He has coached thousands of people in the areas of time and stress management, personal growth, and spirituality. David is a graduate of Trinity University in San Antonio, Texas, where he received his bachelor's degree and a master's degree in teaching. He is the author of Remembering Our Spirit: A Spiritual Survival Guide and is a noted public speaker. He is the father of two wonderful children, is happily married, and lives with his wife in San Antonio, Texas. For more information on David and the services he offers, please go to www.daviddameron.com.

Printed in the United States
22270LVS00004B/1-51

9 781418 466435